Julia C. R. (Julia Caroline Ripley) Dorr

Bermuda. An Idyl of the Summer Islands

Julia C. R. (Julia Caroline Ripley) Dorr

Bermuda. An Idyl of the Summer Islands

ISBN/EAN: 9783743320130

Manufactured in Europe, USA, Canada, Australia, Japa

Cover: Foto ©Andreas Hilbeck / pixelio.de

Manufactured and distributed by brebook publishing software (www.brebook.com)

Julia C. R. (Julia Caroline Ripley) Dorr

Bermuda. An Idyl of the Summer Islands

BERMUDA.

I.

THREE feet of snow, the thermometer at zero, bitter March winds, and remembrances of the slow coming of the New England spring. To sit in the sun and be idle seemed best of all things. But where should we go?

"Now is your time to go to Europe," said our friends, one and all. "The very accepted time. Nothing could be better. You are neither of you good for anything here" (which was very complimentary); "the voyage will set you up, and you will come home new creatures. Telegraph for state-rooms at once."

Europe! The very thought was overpowering. What, then, would the fact be?

Two of us lay awake all night to think of it. We climbed the Alps, veiled our faces before the awful splendor of Mont Blanc, trembled on the verge of dizzy heights, shrank back from fathomless abysses, picked our way across the Mer de Glace, and cowered beneath the weight of the whole incumbent mass of mountains as we went through the tunnel. We wearily traversed miles and miles of picture galleries, stood in damp cathedrals, lifted awestruck faces to more than the Seven Wonders of the World, wandered over battle-fields gay now with yellow wheat and scarlet poppies, visited the shrines of saints and martyrs, museums rich with the storied spoil of ages, and libraries in whose dim alcoves the wisdom and learning of the whole earth was garnered.

In the morning we compared notes, — we two who were ordered off together.

"No, thank you," we said to our friends; "no Europe for us this time. There's too much of it."

"But you need not try to do or to see everything," they answered. "Just go over and settle down somewhere, and take it easy."

"And be forever haunted by the ghosts of lost opportunities," we answered; "tantalized by the daily and nightly thought of what we are missing. We have no strength to waste in vain regrets. We must go somewhere where we can do all there is to do, and all we want to do; where there is enough to interest us, enough to enjoy, and yet where we can be just as lazy as we please without any pricks of conscience. Where, oh where, shall we find this Eden?"

BERMUDA.

We went to Bermuda. The road to Paradise is rough and thorny. Beautiful Bermuda sits upon her coral reefs, guarded by waters that are not to be lightly ventured. Crossing the Gulf Stream diagonally is not conducive to ease of mind or body. Given the passage of the English Channel intensified and stretched out over four days instead of four hours, and you have the voyage from New York to Bermuda. The less said about it the better.

But beyond Purgatory lies Paradise. We left New York on a Thursday in March. On Sunday morning (Easter Sunday of 1883), those of us who were on deck saw a wonderful transformation scene, as the Oronoco passed from the dark and turbulent billows of the Atlantic into the clear blue waters of the land-locked harbor of Bermuda. There was no gradual blending of color. On one side of a sharply defined line was the dull black of molten lead; on the other the bright azure of the June heavens. One by one the white and haggard passengers crept on deck. How they mocked at the delusion of pleasure travel at sea! How they protested that the dry land would be good enough for them after this! Yet in three days' time these same passengers were chartering whale-boats, sail-boats, yachts, steam-tugs, anything that would take them far out among the reefs, where the ocean swell was heaviest. So blessedly evanescent is the memory of sea-sickness!

The Bermudas are a cluster of small islands lying in latitude 32° 20′ N. and longitude 64° 41′ W. They are as far south as Charleston; as far east as Nova Scotia. There is said to be no habitable land so isolated on the face of the round globe, unless it may possibly be St. Helena. Even this possibility is denied by many who claim for Bermuda the supremacy by a few feet or inches. Let some exact statistician get out his little tape measure and decide the momentous question.

The islands lie northeastward to southwestward, in the form of a fish-hook, or a shepherd's crook, twenty-five miles from end to end, and fifteen miles in a straight line. It is claimed that there are three hundred and sixty-five of them, one for each day in the year. But in this count, if count it is, are included many so minute that a single tree would shade their whole circumference. The five largest are St. David's, St. George's, the Main Island, or the Continent, as it is occasionally called, Somerset, and Ireland's Island. St. George's lies at the upper end of the crook; Ireland's at the extreme point. The reputed area of the whole group is only about nineteen square miles!

The islands lie so near each other, the main ones being connected by bridges that span the narrow fiords, that as you approach them you exclaim, "Where are the multitudinous islands? This is surely continuous land." Nature seems to have taken great care of this precious bit of her handiwork. So perfectly is it guarded by its outlying coral reefs that there is but a single channel by which large vessels can enter the harbor. Fifteen miles from shore, at the extreme northern limit of the reefs, rises a picturesque group called the North Rocks, — the highest pinnacles of a submerged Bermuda, — which may itself have been but a mountain peak of the fabled continent Atlantis. But though, according to the chronicle, these rocks may be seen by the approaching traveler, they seldom are, and the first land sighted by the New York steamer is the northeast coast of St. George's Island. By night, the fixed white light on St. David's Head alone gives evidence that land is near. The tortuous, well-buoyed channel can be entered only by daylight.

Out comes the Negro pilot, and scrambles up on deck. We round St. George's, and follow the northern coast line at a respectful distance till we reach Point Ireland and her majesty's dockyard, and come to anchor in Grassy Bay. It is barely noon, but we find to our chagrin that the tide is out, and we must lie here till night and wait for it. Presently appears the little steam-tug, the Moondyne (or Mo-on-dy-nè, — meaning the messenger, — if you choose to appear wiser than other folks), which sooner or later becomes so pleasantly known to all Bermudian visitors, and demands the mail. It is but a five-mile run into Hamilton harbor, and most of the passengers avail themselves of this opportunity to leave the steamer; but the Moondyne, crowded from stem to stern, looks half under water, and the descent by the swaying stairs is not enticing to heads and feet that are still unsteady.

We will take the chances, though hotels be full, and the rule, we are told, "First come, first served."

With our American ideas of the expediency of utilizing the telegraph wires on every possible occasion, adequate or inadequate, it seemed absurd, a going back into the dark ages, to be told in New York that we could not telegraph for rooms. But there is no cable to Bermuda; and the steamer sails only on alternate Thursdays, excepting in April, May, and June. In those three months there is a weekly service. So unless you can make your plans some weeks ahead of your actual journey, you must trust to luck in the matter of quarters.

But would we have dinner? We had forgotten there **was** such a word. **Was** it true, then, that human beings were dependent upon food, **or** at least upon anything beyond a sip of orange-juice and a crumb of biscuit? And could **we** really go downstairs, and sit at a table like Christians?

We went, — a dozen or two of us who had **been raised** from **the** dead that morning; and **by the slow** persuasion of iced claret and sea-biscuit were gradually brought round to the conviction that chicken broth was a good thing, and roast beef was not to be despised.

It is dark when we reach the dock at **Hamilton**, — a dark, rainy, moonless night. How long it takes to lay the planks (after a most primitive fashion), **and** make ready for our disembarkation! Nemo hurries on shore to look **for quarters.** No rooms at the hotels for love or money, but **pleasant** lodgings "out," with board at the Hamilton. A carriage waits, and a not long drive through the soft, damp, odor**ous darkness** brings us to our temporary home.

By a flight of winding stairs outside the house, we reach a covered balcony, over which **a** tropical vine wanders at will. Double glass doors lead into a large, square chamber, with walls of snow and floor of cedar, out of which open two good-sized bedrooms. The furniture is quaint and old-fashioned, and there are brass bedsteads with lace draperies wonderful to behold. On a little odd table between the two windows opposite the door is a great vase, overflowing with roses, lilies white and red, the scarlet-flowering heath, and fragrant branches of rose-geranium.

"Another proof that 'patient waiting is no loss,'" I said.

We learned afterwards that many of our less fortunate shipmates went wandering along the coast for miles that day, in a long search for what we found so easily. There is apt to be a rush when the steamer comes in on Sunday, and some inconvenience until she goes out on Thursday, — taking with her a crowd who leave vacant rooms behind them. Doubtless this will all be remedied after a little, as the course of travel sets more strongly and steadily towards Bermuda. That supply follows demand is a sure rule of political economy.

We crept into blessed beds that would not roll, with a queer but delightful sense of isolation akin to that one feels at night on the highest peak of some lonely mountain. Once on the top of Killington, when the great peak seemed to rock and sway as the strong winds roared around the rocky summit, and the gnarled and weather-beaten fir-trees groaned nd moaned all night long, I had something of the same sensation, — as if I were alone upon some point in space from which I should fall if I stirred. I had not seen Hamilton; had had no glimpse of the town, for even the dock was unlighted. What was Bermuda but a speck, a dot upon the map! Surely the wind that was stirring the cedars would blow us off this atom in the illimitable waste of waters. But we slept, nevertheless.

II.

Two or three low, sweet bugle notes, that I afterwards discovered to be the morning call of the baker's boy, and a burst of jubilant bird-song awakened me. It took but a moment to throw open the window. What a contrast to icy mountains and valleys of drifted snow! Before me were large pride-of-India trees, laden with their long, pendulous racemes of pale lavender, each separate blossom having a drop of maroon at its heart. Clumps of oleanders, just blushing into bloom, rose to the right and the left. Beneath me were glowing beds of geraniums, callas, roses, Easter lilies, and the many-hued coleus. Scarlet blossoms burned against the dark green of the pomegranate leaves. Here rose the tall shaft of a stately palm; there the spreading fans of the palmetto or the slender spires of the swaying bamboo. As far as the eye could reach was one stretch of unbroken bloom and verdure. But stop a minute! Surely there are patches of snow set in all this greenery; snow-covered roofs glittering in the morning sun, and dazzling the eye with their brilliancy. It took more than a glance to discover that the snow was but the white coral rock, of which more anon.

It seemed a cruel waste of time to go to breakfast, but there was no help for it. As we passed from beneath our pride-of-Indias to the winding Serpentine, a very pretty girl, neatly, even daintily, dressed, and carrying a little basket lined with scarlet, tripped up to us, and with a graceful apology for detaining us, in words as well chosen as those of any lady, begged the privilege of doing our washing! The pretty face was dark, — as dark as that of a bronze Venus. We said yes, quite shamefacedly, no doubt, and went our way, wondering what manner of land this might be, where melodious bugle notes announce the advent of the baker, and your washerwoman has the speech and carriage of a duchess.

Truth compels me to say, just here, that the brown beauty did not prove to be an expert laundress, more's the pity. But what ought one to expect of a butterfly? It is not a honey-bee! If her collars and cuffs were not of the orthodox stiffness, and if "doing them up" after her fashion was hardly worth seventy-five cents a dozen, the glimpses she gave us of her pretty, smiling face, and her soft voice and graceful manners as she flitted in and out, were worth a great deal more than that. So we had the best of the bargain, after all. After one week, however, we entrusted our finery to the tender mercies of an older woman, who, if she had no beauty to boast of, gave us good work and entire satisfaction.

But this is a digression. I foresee, already, that digression will be the order of the day in telling this story of our Bermudian days, — those days that were so purposeless, in one sense, and yet so full of the idle content that does not plan, but simply enjoys. We turned to the right or the left, according to the whim of the moment, and all roads led to Rome.

Out to the winding Serpentine, then past the old quarry, up a slight ascent, then a short cut through a rough, steep lane, where two laughing little girls, one white and one black, were always playing, a turn to the right, and we were at the long flight of easy steps, with many levels between, that led to the Hotel Hamilton.

This is a large, commodious building with many pillars and broad verandas, shining in the sun like a palace of white marble. It stands upon a hill, in the midst of pretty and well-kept grounds, overlooking on every side, and the whole year round, a summer landscape, the quaint white-roofed town, and the blue waters of the shining bay. A winding drive, with flights of steps, regular and otherwise, for pedestrians, leads down the somewhat steep descent to the street below. To the right, far off to the southwest, the light-house towers aloft, and by night sends forth the flash of its revolving light once a minute.

But we cannot stand here, held by the glow, the sparkle, the radiant sunshine, and the strange charm of the semi-tropical foliage. Let us go in to breakfast.

The long dining-room was filled with groups of pleasant people, having, on the whole, rather more than the usual *esprit de corps*. Of course there were the "all sorts," that in Bermuda, as elsewhere, it "takes to make a world," and not all were equally agreeable. But were we not all adventurous voyagers, exploring this terra incognita? And did not each new steamer-load of passengers present unknown possibilities? The old inhabitants, many of whom had been there all winter, were ready to extend friendly words of greeting and courteous hospitalities to the new comers, and to put them in the way of enjoying whatever was most enjoyable.

So it happened that a handful of *loquottes* were laid beside my plate that morning, with the remark that they were nearly out of season, and this might be my only opportunity to taste them. The loquotte is somewhat like a yellow plum; bitter and astringent if plucked too soon, but juicy and most delicious when fully ripe.

And so it happened, too, that we were told that very Easter Monday was to be a great day for the boys of Pembroke grammar school. There were to be athletic sports at Tucker's Field, and the victors were to receive their prizes from the fair hands of no less a personage than the Princess Louise. Such an opportunity to see Bermuda in gala-dress was not to be slighted, even if every bone in one's body did ache, and every nerve and muscle quiver; to say nothing of seeing the princess. Of course, in theory, one is quite above any such weakness. But, as a matter of fact, was there ever an American woman who did not want to take a peep at royalty, or its scions, if she had a fair chance?

So to the Field we went, starting early, and taking a long drive to the Flatts on Harrington Sound on the way, in order to call at the quaint and beautiful home of the American consul, Mr. Allen, who has been here for many years. The house is most picturesquely situated just where the waters of the sound pour into the sea through a narrow inlet, spanned by a pretty bridge. Its brick-paved court, with arched entrance, from which winding stairs on the outside of the house lead to the drawing-rooms above, and its overhanging, projecting balconies, give it a singularly foreign aspect that is very charming.

Here we saw our first cocoa-nut palm, its feathery branches making a soft, rustling music as the wind swept through them. And here, too, in the basin of a fountain fed directly from the sea, were dozens of beautiful angel fish, so exquisite in their blue and gold, and with something so human in their mild, innocent faces, that they seemed half uncanny. Here, also, were the little striped "sergeant majors," or pilot-fish. These curious wee creatures seem to be the forerunners, or "pilots," of the mighty sharks, and, it is said, always precede them. Without vouching for the truth of this, I may say that whenever we saw sharks in these waters, as we often did, the pilot-fish invariably preceded them.

Tucker's Field was a gay sight. All Bermuda was there, — a throng of well-dressed, handsome grown folks and pretty children. Full one half were colored people, and it is not too much to say that some of the finest looking and finest mannered of the crowd were among them. One of the most noticeably elegant men on the grounds was a tall and stately black, with a beautiful child in his arms and his pretty wife by his side. There were soldiers in gay coats, streamers and banners flying in the soft yet not heated air, a close greensward under our feet, a wall of cedars encircling us, the blue sky over our heads and glimpses of the blue sea in the distance. Against a background of cedar arose a white pavilion, over which floated the Bermudian flag; and in front of it was a raised platform, covered with scarlet cloth, sacred to the princess and her suite. Her royal highness had not arrived, but the boys were already at their work, running hurdle races, vaulting and leaping.

Presently there was a little commotion, a stir of expectancy. Down sank the British ensign, and the princess's own standard, gorgeous in scarlet and gold, rose in its stead, as an open carriage, with outriders, drove on to the grounds. The princess, in a pretty and simple costume of purple silk, with a bonnet to match,—a little puffed affair, guiltless of flowers or feathers,— bowed to the right and to the left, her strong, sweet, womanly face lighting up as she received the greetings of the people. In Bermuda the Princess Louise won all hearts by her gracious sweetness, her affability, and the cordial kindliness and simplicity with which she met all advances.

But to go back to the boys. They raced; they jumped; they ran "three-legged races;" they rode obstinate though gayly caparisoned donkeys, amid cheers and laughter; they vaulted, the pole being raised higher and higher, until the princess put a stop to it, lest the brave lads should break their necks: and then, one by one, the blushing and victorious knights received their shining silver cups from the hands of her royal highness.

It has been said that courtesy is the rule in Bermuda. Here is a proof of it. At one time during these performances, the crowd surged in front of me, so that I could see only a wall of backs and shoulders. A kindly-faced and sweet-voiced negro woman, perceiving this, touched my shoulder, saying, —

"Take my place, lady. You cannot see."

"But," I answered, "if I do, you will see nothing."

"Oh, that does not matter," she said, with a bright smile. "The lady is a stranger, but I have seen the princess a good many times."

The pretty pageant was over, and our first day in Bermuda as well.

Our first day. But how can I tell of that evening, when we lay in our steamer chairs, on our vine-wreathed balcony, with the soft moonlight irradiating the white roads and the waving palms, casting long shadows everywhere, and touching all things with mystical loveliness?

It was like a dream when we thought of the snow-clad hills we had left six days before, and under the shadow of which our best beloveds were no doubt at that very moment heaping the coal on glowing fires, and saying, "How cold it is!"

But next morning our good landlady said, with a deprecating, apologetic smile, "I don't think you should have sat on the balcony last night. You Americans take risks we Bermudians never think of taking. We think the night air dangerous in winter."

"Winter?" Was this winter? But we did not take cold; and we ran the same fearful risk more than once afterwards, sitting in the moonlight and talking — Nemo and I — of things past, present, and to come.

III.

It had been showery for several days; which means that it had not seemed wise to undertake any long expeditions, though there was really no difficulty in getting about, even on foot. If it rained one minute, the sun shone the next; and so porous is the limestone of the roads that in five minutes after a brisk shower one had no need of overshoes. But no one dreamed of stirring without waterproof and umbrella.

"I have been out four hours this morning," said Flutterbudget, "and was caught in eight showers. But the sun shone most of the time, after all, and it was delightful. What's the use of staying in? One never minds the rain here."

Which was only a fair statement. But we were a little lazy after the rough voyage, and were not sorry for a good excuse to devote ourselves mainly to getting rested, and to writing letters to send back by the Oronoco.

When we caught the last glimpse of her red smoke-stack we turned from the dock, conscious of a new sensation. **It was** as if we were on another planet. Until she should come sailing and steaming back again, we were as absolutely cut off from any communication with home as **if we** were in **the moon.** More **so;** for we could at least see that, — the same full, round moon that was rising slowly over Killington.

Perhaps in this isolation, this fact of being absolutely cut off from one's old life, lies one **of** the chief causes **of** the recuperative power, the restfulness, of a few weeks in Bermuda. For you can't get even a cable dispatch. No matter what happens, — if the bank breaks, or the cashier absconds, if the house burns down, or the children have the measles, or Tom gets married, **or** your favorite candidate **is** defeated, or you yourself are nominated for the presidency, you can't know it for two weeks. Of course there are thoughts of sadder contingencies, as there always must be in life.

But it is astonishing **how** soon one learns to accept the inevitable, and as **a** not unmitigated evil. In some cases it seemed even possible to rejoice at it.

"I positively draw a breath **of** relief every time the steamer sails," said **one** whose life had been spent in the eager stress **and** strain of business, and whose nerves had suffered **therefrom. "It is such a** comfort to know that

I cannot get a letter, or a New York paper, for a fortnight."

By degrees the happy-go-lucky spirit of the islands, which is content to trust to luck and let the world wag as it will, took possession of the wisest of us. And yet I was fain to observe that, notwithstanding all protestations, the five wise virgins and the five foolish ones were equally eager for the mail when once the steamer was signaled!

But one day we found ourselves in what Emery Ann would have called "a regular quandary." Surely it is not necessary in this presence to tell who she was, or *is*, — for if she be not one of the few immortals she is pretty sure to outlive this generation. I have no doubt that when she and Miss Patience Strong took their outing together, sharing both "sights and insights," they found themselves more than once in precisely our predicament.

If we were to stay in Bermuda two months we must have a home, a place where we could gather our belongings about us, make ourselves comfortable, and feel that we were living. I was like a bird without a nest unless so domiciled; and as for Nemo, he had had only an apology for a home since he first went to college, and to have one would be a pleasant change.

But our quarters down the Serpentine had been assigned us only temporarily, with the understanding that we were to have rooms at the hotel, as soon as there were vacancies. Now the Oronoco was on her rolling way back to New York, with her hold full of onions and her staterooms and cabins more than full of passengers; and Hotel Hamilton was naturally desirous to gather her scattered children under her own wing. Yet her vacant rooms happened to be not especially desirable, and for two bedrooms, without a parlor, we would have to pay as much as for our pleasant suite, the balcony and a little store-room included.

Still there were objections to staying where we were. The necessity of putting one's self into street costume at an early hour was in itself a trial to one accustomed to the ease of morning negligee and breakfast caps; and the matutinal repast seemed hardly worth the trouble of going after it.

"How far is it to the hotel, any way?" I asked of Nemo, as we were considering ways and means, with a vague hope that I misapprehended the distance; or that, perhaps, if he said it was but a little way I could stand it.

But he answered, "Well, I should say it was just about as far as to the butternut-tree."

Now to the butternut-tree was a standard

of measurement familiar to all our clan, and "just about" as definite as a piece of chalk. I had always noticed that the distance depended wholly upon one's state of mind. "Only down to the butternut-tree" was but a step, a mere bagatelle, to a band of rosy, laughing children, who flew over the ground like so many young deer in the crisp October mornings, eager to see how many nuts had fallen during the night, and to crack them, all undried as they were, on a certain broad white stone beneath it. Little cared the troop of roguish elves for lips and fingers butternut-brown. But there were circumstances, I had found, under which "'way down to the butternut-tree" lengthened inconceivably.

It seemed to me that the hotel was at least three times as far as to the butternut-tree; and, moreover, it was uphill. But what had I come to Bermuda for but to be out-of-doors, to stray about in the soft sunshine, and to triumphantly disprove the family tradition that I had never learned to walk? Here was my chance, — if, only, one could get rid of the troublesome breakfast question.

To the rescue rushed a kind fairy, who, for a reasonable compensation, would serve me a simple breakfast of bananas, eggs, toast, and tea in my room. So by degrees it settled itself that we were to remain where fate had cast us that first rainy night, in "lodgings out," with board at the Hamilton.

Let me say just here, in case any one who chances to read these pages should have any thought of following our example, that whoever takes any lodging I happened to see will have some things to put up with. Bermuda is not progressive in the way of modern improvements. Very few of the private housekeepers who are willing to rent their rooms to tourists have any idea of many things that we of the North regard not only as conveniences, but as necessities. You will find no bath-rooms with hot and cold water, and you will have to do without other things that at home you think quite indispensable to a well-ordered establishment. Without doubt, most Americans would find themselves more comfortable at some one of the hotels, — the Hamilton being by no means the only one.

But we wanted plenty of room, quiet, and rest. Therefore we made the choice we did, and we never regretted it. To be sure, the chickens disturbed us sometimes of a morning, the cocks sounded their shrill alarum too early, and the birds in the swaying boughs of the pride-of-India trees before my window were occasionally too jubilant. But on the whole order reigned in **Warsaw**, and we were **well** content.

A comfortable rug for the floor **of our** sitting-room, and the loveliest old inlaid table, with two leaves, two cedar-scented drawers, claw feet, and brass toes, giving **us** plenty of room for our books and writing materials, and sundry small, home-like trifles, were gradually added to our furnishings. Gradually, — for everything is done gradually in Bermuda. A transformation that would be brought about in half a **day** by a brisk Yankee housekeeper will require a fortnight here. Why should one hurry when days are long and calm and sweet? Surely there is time enough. The world is not coming to an end, and what is not done to-day can it not be done to-morrow, or the day after?

It was odd to be reminded, in that faraway island of the sea, of Sam. Lawson and Miss Lois's clock. "Some things **can** be druv, Miss Lois, and then agin some things can't, and clocks is that kind. They's jest got **to be** humored." But we were so reminded more than once, before our rooms were settled. **The** one thing that puzzled me in Bermuda, from **first** to last, was to know **who** did the work, and when it was done.

Yet while nobody is in a hurry, and nobody seems to have anything to do, every one is well clad, and looks happy and contented.

IV.

I WANTED a waste-basket, a sponge, and divers other things.

"Go to the Tower," said somebody. "They keep everything there, from a pin to a piano."

It was a clear day at last; not a cloud in the whole wide sky, and the air was like wine. Just to breathe it and to feel one's self alive was enough. The sun was hot, or it seemed so to those of us who were fresh from Greenland's icy mountains; but the breeze from off the sea blew in deliciously, and was as sweet as if it came straight from the shores of Araby the Blest.

Forth we fared — *we* meaning the two of us, Nemo and I — in search of the Tower. It proved to be a substantial building on a conspicuous corner, surmounted by a round tower, from which floated the British ensign. Inside, it is a regular country store, barring perhaps the codfish and molasses. Moreover, it is a book-store, and the headquarters of a circulating library. The proprietor, a naive, courteous, simple-hearted gentleman, — a native Bermudian, — showed us everything we did and did not want, entertained us with pretty stories about the princess, testifying loyally to the grace and benignity of her royal highness, and made not the slightest objection to relieving us of our spare cash, provided it was in good English shillings and sovereigns.

Having made our purchases, we strolled on down the hill to Front Street, where are nearly all the shops and warehouses, the bank, — for there is but one, — and most of the offices and business of the town.

It is a broad, low street, if one may use such an expression, nearly a mile in length, and bordered by a row of pride-of-India trees. These, however, are not in full leaf just now, but are laden with long pendulous blooms, not very unlike our lilac in general appearance, though the racemes are very much less compact, and the flower stems longer. The tree is deciduous, and we do not see it in its glory. In midsummer it casts a dense shade, and the Bermudians have a saying that one need never be hot who owns a pride-of-India tree; that it gathers and holds the coolness, as the cedar-tree holds the heat.

The street is not paved, and the sidewalks do not make a strong impression upon the wayfarer. Pedestrians walk where they will, here, there, or yonder. On one side are the wharves, the docks, the three great iron sheds with their rounded roofs, and below and beyond the shining harbor, alive with sea-craft of all descriptions. White-winged yachts fly hither and thither, fishermen are making ready their swift, strong sail-boats, ferrymen are rowing single passengers, — or a dozen, as the case may be — across to the lovely Paget shore, the Moondyne is getting up steam for a trip through the great sound, and with long steady strokes the blue-jacketed tars of the admiral's ship, the Northampton, send its cutter swiftly over the blue waters.

On the other side of the street are the shops, queer, low, dark, and looking for the most part singularly alike. All have the open piazza in front, two or three yards wide, supported as to its roof, or ceiling, by slender columns. From these piazzas flights of stairs lead to the dwelling-houses above the shops, which are furnished with jalousies, or strong Venetian blinds.

"Onions are up," to-day, — which cabalistic sentence means they are bringing a good price; and from Heyl's Corner, near which is the American consulate, the scene is a gay and a busy one, and the air is filled with the odor of Bermuda violets. A rose by any other name may smell as sweet, but our olfactory nerves fail to perceive that calling **an** onion a violet makes its pungent odor any more delectable. Donkeys, horses, negroes of every age, size, and shade, carts, crates, **sacks,** barrels, and boxes are mingled in seemingly inextricable confusion, and laughter and hilarity abound. There goes a scarlet-coated soldier, and past him strides a tall figure in the green uniform of the Royal Irish Rifles. Yonder a dozen marines are disembarking. Here comes a turbaned negress, balancing a basket of lemons on her head. She **lowers it to** her arm, seemingly without an effort, as we ask her **a** question, smiling and showing teeth as white as milk and even as rows of corn.

The Bermuda lemon looks like **a** large, coarse-skinned orange, being round, and of a deep reddish-yellow in color. It seems, indeed, **to** be **a** cross between the orange and lemon. The pulp-cells are easily separated, and while **a** very sour fruit, which makes a delicious sherbet, it has not the extreme acidity of the lemon of commerce. The trees grow wild and **in profusion,** but the fruit is too short-lived for exportation. We bought four of the great yellow globes for threepence.

On our way home we passed the scene of Mark Twain's great disappointment, and paused for a moment to try to realize his emotions.

There stood the great India-rubber tree, lifting its enormous bole three or four feet from the ground, and at that point dividing into five limbs, each as large as an ordinary tree. It is in private grounds, but as we stood looking meekly over the iron fence we were seen, and courteously invited to walk in for a nearer view. The gardener made a slight incision in the bark to show us the flow of the milk-like sap, and then piloted us through the luxuriant garden and lawns, where many of our carefully tended hot-house plants grow to great size, and orange, pepper, and sago palm-trees flourish. We were hardly able to recognize our "pigeon berry," grown to a stately tree, with a round head, and graceful, drooping branches covered to their very tips with a profusion of yellow berries.

As we passed down one of the avenues the gardener touched a poor little stunted, deformed specimen with his stick.

"A countryman of yours," he said sententiously. "It has given me more trouble than everything else in the garden."

It was an apple-tree.

In the afternoon Nemo went off on a long tramp of investigation, and I strayed away alone, up a still, secluded path, where presently I came to a deep ravine. Down its steep sides grew a plant that seemed new to me. Yet it had a strangely familiar air, and a strong desire seized me to examine its bell-shaped blossoms more closely. But it was out of my reach.

A colored man was washing a wagon at a little distance, and an appeal to him speedily resulted in my possession of the coveted treasures. It was the "life-plant," he said, and it grew everywhere. The leaf is much like that of our "live-for-ever," and it may be a tropical variety of that plant. But it throws up a tall flower-stalk, crowned with a profusion of purplish-crimson bells. If a leaf is pinned to the wall it will at once proceed to grow, throwing out roots, leaves, and even branches. I have never yet heard of one that presumed to bloom under these severe conditions; but leaves that I brought home with me grew and flourished for months, impaled by a barbarous pin.

I was asked long afterwards, on relating this incident, "Were you not afraid, in that wild place, to address a perfect stranger, and a black man at that?"

Perhaps such a thing as discourtesy may be known on the islands. I speak only from my own experience and observation. Manners, if not hearts, are exceedingly friendly. Everybody, as a rule, salutes. No man, be he white or black, passes a lady without lifting his hat. Every child makes its grave little salutation.

Negro women with baskets on their heads give you a word or smile, as they go by. Little boys and girls steal shyly up with gifts of flowers or fruit. If you ask a question it is courteously answered; if you beg a favor it is immediately granted. If you look wistfully over a garden fence, you are invited in, and you depart laden with fragrant spoils.

To have any fear of anything or anybody seems as absurd as it is impossible.

V.

PERHAPS there is poverty in Bermuda, but squalor and absolute want, if they exist, keep themselves strangely out of sight. The first thing, perhaps, that strikes the visitor, after the beauty of the water and the perfection of the flowers, is the appearance of ease and well-to-do comfort that pervades the islands. There is no rubbish, no dirt, no dust, no mud. Instead of the tumble-down shanties that deform and defile the rest of the world, here the humblest citizen not only dreams of marble halls, but actually dwells in them, — or seems to. All the houses are built of the native snow-white stone, a coral formation that underlies every foot of soil. When first quarried, this stone is so soft that it can be cut with the knife. But it hardens on exposure to the air, and so durable is it that a house once builded is good for at least a hundred years. Every man seems to be the owner of a "quarry," so called. He who wishes to build him a house has but to scrape off a foot or two of the red surface soil, and lo! there lies his building material ready to his hand, or rather to his saw. No blasting is required, no slow, laborious drilling, no vast expenditure of time and money, such as has made so many Vermont marble quarries the mausoleums of dead hopes and buried treasure.

But if money does not go into the opening of these Bermuda quarries, so neither does it come out of them — to any great extent; which certainly goes far to equalize matters.

The stone is sawed by hand into cubes, perhaps two feet long, one foot wide, and one foot thick. These are piled like bricks, with interstices between for the circulation of the air, and left to dry. The vacant space made by the removal of the rock forms the cellar, which is thus already walled and floored, and the builder has only to go on and put up his house. Thin, flat slabs of the same stone, placed at a slight slope, form the roof, and this is whitewashed periodically, so that the seemingly snow-covered roofs of Bermuda strike the eye at once, and are in strong contrast to the deep verdure in which they are set.

That this coral formation, which is really a species of limestone, readily lends itself to architectural purposes is shown by the really beautiful interior of Trinity Church, or the Cathedral, as it is otherwise called. This edifice is well off for names, for it is also styled a

"Chapel of Ease," whatever that may mean ; I confess I do not know. But it is a fine building, with a very deep chancel, on either side of which (outside the railing) are ranged stately pews for the accommodation of the dignitaries, civic, military, and ecclesiastic. Several handsome memorial windows add to its dignity and give pleasure to visitors.

A certain air of indescribable quaintness and simplicity seemed nevertheless to pervade the place, and touched me not a little. In the vestibule hung a tablet with a pathetic inscription. I wish I could give it verbatim, but I can only make an approach to it, —

"Oh, thou who enterest this holy place, depart not till thou shalt have offered up a prayer, not only for thyself and thy dear ones, but for all those who worship here."

(I leave the above paragraph, unaltered — as a flower dropped by a stranger above the ashes of Trinity. But on the 10th of February, 1884, the beautiful church was destroyed by fire. It is a loss to the small community that can scarcely be measured.)

The stately villas of Mount Clare and Woodlands and the fine new house of General Hastings at Fairyland also display the capabilities of this stone, as well as the handsome and massive gateways, with their arches and columns, that one meets at every turn. These, with the well-kept grounds, give an impression of affluence and elegance that is, perhaps, sometimes misleading. For we are told that there are not many large incomes in Bermuda, and that the style of living in these beautiful and picturesque homes is very simple and unostentatious.

It is the very afternoon for a walk, the air being cool and bracing, though the sun is hot. It is the 3d of April, and the mercury at eight A. M. stood at 62° in the shade. "Too cold to work out-of-doors," explained a laborer whom our landlord had engaged to work in his garden; and forthwith he gathered up his tools and departed. Think of that, ye Yankee farmers, who chop wood and "cut fodder" with the thermometer at zero!

Shall we go to the North Shore, taking Pembroke church by the way? You can see its square tower of massive stone rising above the trees yonder. The long white roof with the two towers, nearly opposite, just beyond that stately royal palm, belongs to Woodlands, one of the finest places here. Here the hard, smooth road leads us on between long avenues of cedar-trees, and there between walls of coral rock thirty feet high. We pause to rest on a low stone wall, where the oleander hedges, just bursting into bloom, pink and white and vivid crimson, reach far above our heads and fill the air with fragrance. Deadly sweet? Poisonous? May be so, like many other charming things. **But we'll risk it,** with **this** strong sea-breeze blowing.

We meet funny, sturdy little donkeys drawing loads preposterously large ; carts laden with crates of onions for the outgoing steamer ; negro women bearing baskets and bundles on their turbaned heads, — tall, erect, stately, oftentimes with strong, clearly cut features almost statuesque in their repose ; children, white and black, just out of school, with their books and satchels.

For **a** wonder, the square-towered Pembroke **church** is closed. But the gate is open, and **we turn** into the **quiet** churchyard, where so **many** generations lie buried. To unaccustomed eyes the scene **is a** strange one, and the effect is most singular. The surface of the ground is almost hidden **by** gray, coffin-shaped tombs, like huge sarcophagi, solid and heavy as the eternal rocks of the island. As I understand **it,** the bodies are deposited, tier upon tier in many cases, **in** excavations, **or** tombs, cut **in** the underlying rock ; and these strange structures are **raised** over them. But the impression one gets is that of **a** multitude of great stone coffins resting on the ground. Very few of them bear any inscription. For the most part, they are simply numbered, and the record of names and dates is kept in a parish book.

This custom — to which of course there are exceptions, as in the case of Bishop Field, who lies under a slab of Peterhead granite, suitably inscribed — has its disadvantages. For instance: I was told that on the death of the sexton, or clerk, who had charge of one of these books of record, his wife claimed the book as her own private property, and demanded the sum of twenty pounds as indemnity for giving it up. The parish refused to recognize her claim, and the woman in a fit of passionate rage destroyed the precious volume.

This may not be true. I do not vouch for it. But *if* true, it must have been painful and tragic, as well as inconvenient.

But love is the same everywhere, and cares for its dead all the same.

Palms rustle softly. Pride-of-India trees, oleanders, and pomegranates wave their boughs and scatter their blossoms. Lilies and callas and roses in rich profusion make the place lovely beyond description, while wreaths and crosses lie upon tombs that are gray with age. At the head of one grave — that of Governor Laffan, who died last year — is a great tub of English violets. At its foot a sago-palm stretches its broad arms as if in benediction.

We go past the government house, Mount Langton, catching a glimpse of the avenue, where the *bourganvilier*, a tropical vine, covers a wall thirty-five feet high with a solid mass of crimson flowers. But special permission to enter must be had; so we can only take a surreptitious glance to-day, and are soon at the North Shore, looking straight out to sea.

The nearest point of land is Cape Hatteras, six hundred and fifty miles away. The strong ocean winds, free from all taint of earthly soil or sin, sweep over us with strength and healing in every breath. And the coloring! Look! Far off on the horizon, the sky, azure overhead, softens to a pale rose-color. The line that meets it is a deep indigo blue, — a blue so intense that we can hardly believe it is the sea. Thence, through infinite gradations, the color faints and fades, from indigo to dark sapphire, from sapphire to lapis-lazuli, from lapis-lazuli to the palest shade of the forget-me-not. It changes, even as we gaze, to deepest emerald, which in turn fades to a tender apple-green, touched here and there with rose. It dies away in saffron and pale amber, where it kisses the shore, with long reaches of purple where the coral reefs lie hidden.

But as we scramble down upon the rocky shore, how the huge breakers foam and fret! They toss their proud heads, and dash themselves against the frowning cliffs with the noise of booming thunder. We can scarcely hear our own voices, and will run from the spray and the tumult to a quieter spot farther on. Here we find some oddly shaped shells, and that strange creature called the Portuguese man-of-war. It looks like a pale bluish pearl, shining in the sun; but it is merely an elliptical bladder, and floats about, balanced by long, blue, hanging tentacles. Capture it with cane or parasol if you can; but beware of touching it, for it exudes a subtle liquid that will sting you like a nettle.

"Halloo!" cried Nemo, exultingly. "I've caught them, — two of them! Come down and see how pretty they are, — like fairy boats."

I was sitting under the lee of a high wall, sharing, with serene indifference, the wind's sharp tussle with my veil and bonnet strings. But I managed to scramble down the rocks again.

"'Boat?'" said I. "It is for all the world like a shoe, — a little glass shoe. It is Cinderella's own slipper! But what are you going to do with them?"

"Take them home and see if there is any

way to preserve the things. See the lovely iridescent blue tint, like a bit of the sky!"

"And see how deftly they are laced, like other shoes," I said. "Put them in your handkerchief, and come on, Nemo. They'll collapse in a minute."

But they did not. One of them dried perfectly, retaining its shape and much of its exquisite coloring.

We wandered home across a field or two and through a pleasant grove, from which a rough path leads to a high hill which we must climb some day, coming out into Cedar Avenue again, through a slit in the stone wall just opposite Pembroke.

After dinner Mr. T. introduced us to a porcupine fish, — a curious creature, with formidable-looking quills, but a most innocent and infantile expression of countenance.

"When I caught it," said Mr. T., "I had much ado to keep from chucking it under the chin, it looked so like a baby."

VI.

HAVING been to the North Shore yesterday, it should certainly be in order to-day to cross the island to the Sand Hills, on the South Shore, — shortening the distance, if we choose, by taking the ferry across the harbor to Paget. The ferry is a row-boat, and Charon will take us over for a penny ha'penny apiece, with all the beauty and the soft sweet airs thrown in. Cheap enough, in all conscience! For here are softly undulating shores, green-clad hills, white cottages, — each a pearl in setting of emerald, — the busy dock with its quaintly foreign aspect, the white-winged yachts flying hither and thither, the blue sky overhead, the bluer sea below. Is it not worth the money? Yonder lies a Norwegian ship, with her sailors climbing the shrouds like so many monkeys. Round the nearest point comes a boat from H. M. ship Tenedos. The Tenedos is lying at Grassy Bay, making herself fine to receive the princess, and her jolly tars are in high spirits. When her royal highness sails, next week, what with the flying banners and the gayly dressed crowd, the blue and white canopy with its flower-wreathed pillars, the broad scarlet-covered steps leading down to the water, the admiral's cutter with its blue-jacketed tars, the gold-laced admiral himself with his sword and his plumed hat and all the rest of the fuss and feathers, it will be for all the world like a scene from Pinafore.

But this morning Jack is bent on getting rid of his money. He will manage to leave half a year's wages behind him in those queer, dark, uninviting little shops on Front Street. For there are more enticements hidden away in most incongruous nooks and corners than one would imagine. You step into a grocery, for instance, and find a fine display of amber jewelry. If you are in want of some choice cologne, do not fail to ask for it at the nearest shoe-shop. It is as likely to be there as in more legitimate quarters. The rule is, If you want a thing, hunt till you find it. It is pretty sure to be somewhere.

A pleasant walk from the ferry brings us to the Sand Hills, over which we tramp, only pausing to admire the exquisite oleander blooms, the largest we have yet seen. We clamber down the rocks, and reach the long, smooth white beach, as hard and level as a floor. There is a fresh breeze, and the surf comes rolling in, driving the baby crabs far up the beach, and leaving them stranded. We laugh at their queer antics for a minute, and then leave them to chase the sea-bottles that are rolling over the sand. Can they really be alive, these little globes of iridescent glass filled with sea-water?

But we turn, erelong, from all the strange creatures of the sea to the sea itself, lured by its own resistless spell. There is not a being in sight, save one lone darkey gathering mussels in the distance. There is not a sign of human habitation; only the long stretch of sandy beach, the rocky background, and the wide ocean, vast, lonely, illimitable. We write dear names on the sand, and with half a smile and a whole sigh watch the tide as it blots them out. What do we care that myriads before us have played at the same childish game? Higher and still higher up we write them, but the result is always the same. The cruel, crawling, hungry sea stretches its hand over them, and they are gone.

Nemo wanders off, after a while, to interview the darkey, and inquire into the details of the traffic in mussels. The wind is blowing briskly; the tide is rolling in from far beyond the reefs over which it foams and frets. I sit on one rock, under the shelter of another, and fancy flies fast and far into "the **dark backward and abysm of time.**"

For here on this very South Shore, tradition saith, did Ariel leave the king's son, Ferdinand, —

> "Cooling **of the** air with sighs
> In an odd angle of the isle, and sitting,
> His arms in this sad knot."

Here, **too,** did the tricksy sprite assure **his** master that

> "Safely in **harbor**
> Is the king's ship; in the deep nook, where once
> Thou call'dst me up at midnight to fetch dew
> From the still-vexed Bermoothes, there she's hid."

How appropriate **is** this epithet one can scarcely understand until he has seen the chafing **of** the sea over the rugged rocks and reefs that **in** Shakespeare's time were thought to **be** the abode of monsters and devils. Where was Prospero's cell? Where slept the fair Miranda? Upon what bank sat Ferdinand when **Ariel sang,** "Come unto **these** yellow sands"?

> "Full fathom five thy father lies;
> Of his bones are coral made;
> Those are pearls that were his eyes:
> Nothing of him that doth fade
> **But** doth suffer a sea-change
> Into something rich and strange."

Hark! Who knows but the sweet, low music of the waves owes half its magic to the spell of Ariel's remembered song? Where dwelt the "foul witch, Sycorax"? and in which of these caverns, the very darkest and wildest of them all, was the lair of Caliban?

With some handsome crab-shells, and two or three "sea-bottles," — curious little bladders filled with sea-water, looking precisely like glass marbles of palest amber, — we climbed the rocks again, and wandered back to the thicket of oleanders. The blooms were of immense size, and of every gradation of color, ranging from purest white, through all the intermediate shades of pink, to deepest crimson.

"From this day forth," I said, "deliver me from a stunted oleander, growing in a ten-inch pot, and tormented by scaly-bugs."

It is an unwritten law in Bermuda that one should always go by one road and return by another. Rather than break it we strolled on, following a wall that led — somewhere. Pretty soon a youngster of ten pattered up behind us, and gravely answered our salute, looking at us askance from under his broad-brimmed palmetto hat. Under the beguiling influence of a penny, however, he soon grew communicative; and presently confided to us the story of his woes. He had not had so much as a glimpse of the princess! and she was going away in a few days! All the rest of the family had seen her; but even on the day of her reception at St. George's he had to stay at home to mind the house. Poor little man! and there might never be a princess in Bermuda again.

"But," he added, as if to console himself, "they say she dresses very plain!"

"Is it possible?" said I. "I thought a princess had rings on her fingers and bells on her toes, and that, if she were a very great princess indeed, she wore some kind of a crown. Is n't that so?"

"Oh, no!" he said, half under his breath. "Why, they say she goes shopping in calico!"

To appreciate this one should have heard the emphasis on the last word. But having thus delivered himself, he brightened up, and began pegging stones at a bluebird.

A familiar plant grew by the wall, but by one of memory's perverse tricks I could not recall the name of it.

"What is that, my boy?" I asked, touching it with my parasol. "What do you call it?"

"Flannel plant," said he.

"What?" I repeated.

"Flannel plant."

"Is that what your mother calls it?"

"Yes 'm."

"Behold how language changes and degenerates," said Nemo, picking a bunch of aromatic fennel. "When this boy's great-grandmother came over from Old England, and brought a root of her favorite herb with her, doubtless she called it fennel. Fennel, fannel, flannel; there you have it."

The urchin listened with wide eyes. Then as we reached the parting of the ways, he dashed round a corner and disappeared.

Ten minutes afterwards, as we passed a little shop at the cross-roads, we saw him standing in the doorway eating a stick of striped candy. That penny had burned a hole in his pocket. Boy nature is pretty much the same everywhere.

We came out near the pretty Paget church, rested for a while under a palm-tree, and then strolled on down the shaded road to the ferry, which we recrossed in time to dress for dinner.

Our balcony looked very cool and inviting. Within, the great, white, shadowy room was fragrant with masses of roses and lilies. You can't buy flowers in Bermuda; but its whole world is ready to give them to you, if you are known to love them, without money and without price.

"I believe I am tired," I said, sinking into an easy-chair. "Nemo, give me one of those shell-roses to comfort myself with."

"Lady Mither, do you know you have walked more than three miles? What would they say at home?"

VII.

Did I say it would be like a scene from Pinafore? It was! They were all there, Ralph Rackstraw, Sir Something Somebody, K. C. B., the able-bodied seamen from the Queen's Navee, and the whole crowd, uncles and brothers, as well as the sisters, the cousins, and the aunts. One had but to close one's eyes to the surroundings, — but to shut out the atmosphere, — and the little pavilion became the stage at which we have all looked more than once. Only the footlights were missing.

The Oronoco was lying at her dock, very near the flight of stone steps from which her royal highness was to embark, and a large party of us secured good places on her upper deck, which overlooked the blue-canopied pavilion. For it was impossible not to catch a little of the enthusiasm that thrilled the hearts of the loyal Bermudians. We laughed slyly at ourselves, and good-naturedly at each other; but nevertheless we all went to see the show.

And a pretty show it was. Not grand, nor imposing; but under that blue sky, with the clear sunshine irradiating all things and making the sea, that was bluer even than the sky, glow and sparkle with wonderful intensity; with flags flying from every housetop and window, and fluttering from every mast-head; with sail-boats gliding hither and yon like so many white-winged birds; with the red coats of the soldiers and the blue jackets of the sailors making picturesque bits of color here and there; with the eager, expectant faces, black and white; the restless, impatient children, the flowers and the streamers, it was a pretty sight and well worth seeing.

From our perch on the Oronoco we could look down into the flower-wreathed pavilion which had been erected at the head of the broad flight of stairs leading down from the dock to the water. On either side of it rose tiers of seats, one above another, for the accommodation of the insular dignitaries. These slowly filled even to the topmost row. Carriages dashed hither and thither. There was a sound of distant music, and down the street from Prospect filed the long ranks of the Royal Irish Rifles, in dark green uniforms picked out with white, and drew up in line across the street. Round the point swept the admiral's cutter, rowed by eight oarsmen, and drew up at the foot of the stairs.

And still we waited. The pavilion itself was empty, save for one old man with a broom, who persistently swept and smoothed the scarlet cloth, with broad border of blue, that covered every inch of the floor and steps. Evidently there would be no shred of lint, no speck of dust, to profane the unwonted dignity of that carpet while he was to the fore!

Finally appeared his honor the mayor, then his excellency Lieutenant-General Gallway, governor and commander-in-chief; and shortly after, the admiral, Sir John Edmund Commerell, V. C., K. C. B., in full uniform, with his cocked hat, plumed and gold-laced, and all the paraphernalia of his office.

But still we waited. Her royal highness was to have sailed at half past two, and it was now three.

"The Princess Louise has not her mother's business-like promptness," said a gentleman near us. "Nobody ever has to wait for the Queen."

At length a carriage came sweeping round the curve of the bay. All eyes turned in that direction, and the green uniforms opposite were on the alert. It was not the princess, but it was the ladies of her suite. And finally she appeared, the observed of all observers, clad in olive browns from tip to toe. There was not much cheering. The crowd was a very silent one. It seemed to a looker-on that hearts were a little too full for noisy demonstration. The feeling of Bermuda for Louise was more than simple loyalty. It was real affection. The island had taken her to its very heart.

But now the end had come. His honor made his little speech,—which was quite inaudible from our stand-point,—a little girl presented a big bouquet nearly as tall as herself, Governor Gallway paid his devoirs, and then the princess made her farewells, shaking hands with every one who approached her, high or low, black or white, and seeking out many who did not venture to seek her.

The admiral was just about handing her into the boat, when she saw standing at the head of the stairs, with disappointment visible in her face, an elderly lady in black who had in some way been overlooked in the adieux. Turning quickly, she ran back up the long flight like a school-girl, took the old lady's hand and held it while saying a few words that will surely never be forgotten, then ran down again, and stepped lightly into the boat.

Oars flashed in the sun, the cutter flew over the shining waves, and in a few moments we saw a lithe brown figure ascending the ladder of the Supply, which, convoyed by the whole fleet of yachts, moved slowly down the harbor. The Tenedos, in which the princess was to sail, lay in waiting at Grassy Bay. There was much waving of handkerchiefs, there were cries of "Good-by! good-by!" and "God bless her!" but there were no shouts or cheers. Bermudian annals will long make mention of "the year the princess was here."

The air was full of stories about her, and her relations to the people, all that season. Some were pretty, and some were funny; and many of them were repeated and garbled by industrious and adventurous reporters, till they bore scarce a trace of resemblance to the facts. But that Louise was greatly attracted to, and amused by, the colored people, and that she delighted to enter their houses and talk to them, is undoubtedly true, whether she ironed old Mammy's shirts or not. She enjoyed to the full the rare freedom of her life in the island, its lack of conventional restraints, and the simplicity and warm-heartedness of the people. She went among them with little or no formality, inviting herself to lunch with them and to join, at times, in their festivities; merging, as it were, the princess in the lady. She drove about in a little basket phaeton, and went "shopping in calico," providing for her small *ménage* like any other housekeeper. A laughable story is told of a tradesman of whom she asked the price of some trifle.

"Our price, your royal highness," he said, — "our price is three shillings. But to *you* we shall make it two-and-nine!"

"Even the birds call me 'Louise,' in Bermuda," she wrote to a friend.

Which only proves that the cardinal grosbeak is the most arrant trifler that ever made love to trusting hearts. I am positive that he was continually calling "Julie! Julie!" in the very sweetest and most persuasive accents; and numberless other women are ready to swear that their names were the sole burden of his song. What shall be done to him? for he is the veriest rogue and madcap that ever flashed like a scarlet flame from tree to tree. He fairly lights up the landscape with his brilliant plumage, while his constant companions, the bluebirds, are like bits of the sky itself, — such an intense and exquisite blue as is seldom seen.

Very beautiful, too, are the dainty little ground doves, — diminutive creatures scarcely larger than your thumb, clad in Quaker gray, and as demure as their garb. They are seen everywhere, in pairs and in flocks, bowing and cooing and picking their way about in the very daintiest fashion. I never happened to see one on the wing, — though of course they fly, like other doves.

There are many other birds, casual or accidental visitors from far-off shores, and migratory in their habits. But these are at home on the island, and so overshadow all the others that one scarcely notices them. A few other varieties remain through the year.

St. Patrick must some time have visited Bermuda, for snakes are unknown. The nearest approach to a reptile is the turtle, and one or two varieties of lizards. Spiders are numerous, and occasionally one sees a veteran of exceedingly large proportions, — a regular Daniel Lambert of a spider, — who will peer down at you from over your door, or suddenly appear to you at dead of night silhouetted on the white wall of your chamber, in rather startling fashion.

But though not exactly agreeable comrades, they are entirely harmless, and one soon learns not to mind their antics. We were in an old house, too, where perhaps they throve better than in newer quarters.

It is said there is not a poisonous plant or a venomous insect in Bermuda, unless one may call mosquitoes venomous. Yet, in the case of plants, especially, it is hard to understand how or why this should be. No plants seem to be indigenous there, but all were conveyed thither by natural or artificial means. Why this conveyance should have been restricted to such as were not harmful it is not easy to see. When the island was discovered it had but one variety of tree, — the cedar, or juniper, which is even yet more numerous than all the rest combined.

The little blue Bermudiana, a larger growth of our familiar "blue-eyed grass," stars the ground everywhere; the trailing crab-grass clothes it in perennial green; the wild sage-bush meets you at every turn. I was quite in love with a pretty thistle, with sage-green leaves and a single flower of pale-lemon color, that grows by the waysides. The rose-geranium is as common and as hardy as our mayweed. And oh, wonder of wonders, — callas and caladiums, the pets and dainty darlings of our greenhouses, grow in out-of-the-way corners, seemingly at their own wild will! I must say, however, that I thought the former not so delicate and beautiful as when grown in pots, as with us. They bear no comparison to the wonderful Easter lilies of Bermuda.

VIII.

It is Sunday morning, and all eyes are turned anxiously to the signal station of Mount Langton. As we look, a red-white-and-blue pennant flies from the yardarm, announcing that the steamer from New York is in sight. Now we can go to church in peace, sure of getting our mail some time to-morrow. It is impossible to get it to-day, and after a little natural Yankee grumbling at Bermudian slowness we accept the situation. What does it matter? What does anything matter in this lazy, lotus-eating land, where it seems always afternoon?

The Bermudians are a church-going people. The question asked is not, "*Are* you going to church to-day?" but, "*Where* are you going?" The going is taken for granted, as it used to be in New England. Yet there is no Puritanic sombreness. All is gay and bright. Flags fly in honor of the day from Mount Langton, from Admiralty House, and from the shipping in the harbor. At half past nine A. M. precisely a pennant flies from the staff in Victoria Park, to announce that church time is near.

We Hamiltonians can go to Pembroke, beautifully set in its garden of green; or to Trinity, a handsome church, with fine memorial windows, and columns and arches of the native stone. Or we can get Charon to row us across the ferry, and stroll for a mile along a quiet, shaded country road to the beautiful Paget church. If we do this last, we shall surely be tempted to rest a while on a low stone wall that runs parallel with the road behind the parish school, and try to fix the lovely picture in our minds forever.

We can easily find a Presbyterian kirk and a Wesleyan chapel. But here, as in England, Dissenters are in the minority, the union of church and state being very close. Surgeon General John Ogilvy, in a little pamphlet issued last year, gives the following table showing the religious preferences of the inhabitants, according to the census of 1881: —

Church of England	10,003
Wesleyan	1,672
Methodist Episcopal	752
Roman Catholic	391
Reformed Episcopal	208

Wherever we go, however, we shall find the same pleasant and cordial mingling of whites and blacks in the audience. Bermuda does not raise a partition wall between her children, setting the light on one side, the dark on the other. Their pews are side by side in the flower-decked churches, and as a rule the colored people are as neatly dressed, as well mannered, and as devout as their lighter brethren. One cannot look upon their tranquil, thoughtful faces, or hear their low-toned, musical voices in the responses, without thanking God for what fifty years of freedom, under favorable auspices, can do for the black race.

Just here I beg to make a short extract from Dr. Ogilvy : —

"The colored people of the island are the descendants of the old negro and American Indian slaves, much intermingled with white blood, and are gradually, by their energy and wish to improve themselves, by schooling and otherwise, taking up a better position with regard to the whites. They are also slowly acquiring the ownership of patches of land, and dotting the country with their cottages of lime-washed stone. The rural population is, perhaps, better housed than in most countries. This is favored by the continual subdivision of the land into small parcels. . . . The still higher development of the colored race may be looked for in the not distant future. Even now their ambition aspires to a share in the administration, although caste prejudices are still strong, even amongst **the different strata** of the European residents. At least one **member of the** House of Assembly is a colored man."

Dr. Ogilvy refers to the energy of the race, and to their wish to improve themselves **and** their condition. His position as principal medical officer, Bermuda Command, gives him unquestionable facilities for knowing whereof **he** speaks. It is the fashion, however, to say that the blacks are lazy and shiftless; a state**ment** that, **as** far as a mere observer could judge, does not seem to be exactly warranted by the facts. Certainly their houses are as good as those of the lower class of whites, and in many cases very much better; their little fields **are** as well tilled, and they themselves are as well clothed and as well fed. I was told that they were more eager than the working classes among the whites to avail themselves of **all** the privileges of the schools for their children.

As for their "laziness," everybody is lazy in Bermuda, speaking from a New England point of view; but it is a very charming laziness, and **it** remains to be proved that the blacks are any more fond of taking their ease **than** are their white brethren. It is in the very **air.** The land is a lovely, dreamy, restful land, and to expect of its children the push and "go-ahead-a-tive-ness" of a typical Yankee is to expect impossibilities.

A little good-natured laughter may be allowed when one discovers that a tradesman, getting a little tired of the pressing cares of business, simply locks his door and goes off to recreate for a longer or shorter period, as the case may be. One may smile at the fabulous story of the commission merchant who still keeps open doors, — if the sun shines, — and who thinks he does a good business though he has not had a fresh consignment of goods since 1858! But most of us have two strains of blood in our natures. The wide-awake, stirring northern current might rebel after a while, at the easy, careless, happy-go-lucky life of these islands. I rather think it would, in most cases. But it suits the sensuous southern strain to a charm; and as most of us came here for rest and recuperation, why should we quarrel with it? Why should we not take the good the gods provide, and be therewith content? If we can carry home with us a little Bermudian repose to engraft upon the stock of our American restlessness and feverish excitability, the fruit our trees will bear in the next generation may, perhaps, be all the sweeter.

Bermuda belongs to the see of Newfoundland and Labrador, the bishop making a yearly visitation. What a rounding **of the** circle, — to **live half** the year in frozen Labrador, and half in soft Bermuda!

There are nine parishes, with the names of which the visitor soon grows as familiar as with the streets of his native town; if he stays long he talks of St. George's, Hamilton Parish, Smith's Parish, Devonshire, Pembroke, Paget, Warwick, Southampton, and Sandys as glibly as the islanders themselves. Hamilton Parish, however, must not be confounded with the town of Hamilton, which is in the parish of Pembroke. Each parish has its own church, but it is often the case that one clergyman officiates in **two** parishes, holding service in one in the forenoon and in the other in the afternoon or evening. Wherever we went we found the music good, the services conducted with great reverence and decorum, and the attendance what we should consider exceptionally large in proportion to the number of inhabitants. Crowds of children, both white and colored, running and walking hand in hand, neatly dressed, and with happy, smiling faces, thronged **the Sunday-schools.**

It strikes one singularly to hear in this remote dot **in** the boundless seas that schools and public libraries were introduced as far **back as 1631;** and that under the influence of

Oliver Cromwell, Lord Protector, **church** matters excited general interest, — Sabbath-breaking, intoxication, *witchcraft*, and other offenses being punished with Puritanical rigor. Shade **of** Cotton Mather! Who can believe it?

Yet we are told, too, that the first Methodist minister who was sent from England to Bermuda, in 1799, was received with great intolerance, and **was** submitted to persecution and imprisonment. This state of things lasted but a short time, however, and there are now nine Wesleyan churches, one Methodist Episcopal, **two** Presbyterian, **one** Reformed Episcopal, and one Roman Catholic.

Variety enough for nineteen sparsely settled **square miles!** Bermuda would have afforded a beautiful field for the establishment of the **one** Broad Church of which **we** dream. But it must needs follow the fashion, and weaken **its** strength by splitting itself up into diverse and opposing sects, like all the rest of the world.

Parliament is composed of a legislative and executive council, appointed by the crown, and **an** assembly. The latter, formed of four members from each **parish, is elected for** a term of seven years. The schools are in **charge of the** parish authorities, who **are** empowered to enforce attendance. A fine is exacted from the parent if the child fails to appear. There are also several private schools, which are said to be good. At all events, the Bermudians are refined and intelligent, and by far the greater number, of course, have been educated at home. Now and then the son or daughter of a well-to-do family is sent to England to be "finished," but one meets many bright and clever men and women who have never left the islands.

Several attempts have been made to establish a college, or classical school of a high grade, but they seem to have come to naught. It is said that the public schools have much to contend with in the absence of thoroughly trained teachers, — a want not easily filled so far from the sources of supply.

Slavery, which was established about the year 1618, and which had been a gentle bondage from the first, was abolished in 1834, without the usual term of apprenticeship. There were at that time 4,200 slaves in the islands. England paid the owners at the rate of about seven pounds for each slave, — certainly not an exorbitant sum for flesh and blood, with the soul thrown in, if it is worth anything. But emancipation proved an entire success. Most of the slaves were greatly attached to their masters, and they all received the gift of freedom with absolute equanimity.

IX.

I FOUND myself continually wondering how life looked, what the wide world was like, to eyes that had seen nothing but blue seas, blue skies, perpetual summer, and the narrow spaces of this island group. What impressions do they form of vast, silent, lonely prairies, almost as limitless as their ocean reaches? what of towering mountains and far-stretching continents? How do they picture snow and hoar-frost, — like wool? How do they dream of crowded cities, single streets of which give shelter to more inhabitants than those of all Bermuda? Cathedrals, temples, towers, and palaces, — the whole domain of art and recondite learning, with its galleries, its libraries, its museums; the world of humanity, with its large charities, its vast enterprises, its commerce that binds nations together in bonds of common interest, — how can they grasp them all?

It would be strange if a certain insular narrowness were not sometimes to be felt, as when a lady said to her friend, "I wonder what the world would do without Bermuda! Just think how many potatoes and onions we export!"

A bright little girl said to me, "I would like to visit you. If ever I go to America, I would seek to find your house."

What comprehension could she have of any place, or any state of society, in which it would not be easy to find the way to the house of any friend?

It is a blessed fact that one's own home is the hub of the universe. Bermuda does not seem small to its inhabitants. To them it is the world, and holds the fullness thereof. "The maps do not do us justice," said one of them to the writer. "For you see we really are not so very small."

But the truth is that in its exceeding smallness lies one of its chief charms. And to realize how small it is one must visit the lighthouse, a drive of six miles, or so, from Hamilton. Down the hill to Front Street, past Parliament House and the Public Library, past Pembroke Hall and its group of Royal Palms, — five magnificent trees, lifting their stately, granite-colored shafts like columns in some ancient temple, — round the harbor, and then on through Paget and Warwick to Gibbs's Hill in Southampton. This is one of the most delightful drives possible, the road running past fine country mansions and cosy cottages, with here and there a glimpse of the shining sea. Just where we leave the highway to go to Gibbs's Hill we pass a ruined house, weird and sombre in its desolation. It is a place to haunt one's dreams. The high stone steps are worn in great suggestive hollows. The water tank is empty, and rats have taken possession. From the broken windows ghostly faces seem peering out. But we pick a geranium that flaunts gayly in the sun by the shattered door-sill, and go on our upward and winding way to the light-house.

All one has to do to make a cutting grow in Bermuda is to stick it in the ground,—either end up! It seemed to make little difference which. On returning home that night I put the slip from the "ruined-house geranium" in a pot of lilies on the balcony. It took root immediately, and is growing to-day under the shadow of snow-clad hills. What does it think of them, I wonder?

Up and up we go until we reach what is next to the highest point on the islands. Yet Gibbs's Hill, which enjoys this amazing altitude, is only 245 feet above high-water level. The light-house is a massive tower of stone, filled in with concrete, 130 feet high. From the deck of a ship, forty feet from the water, the light can be seen about **thirty-three** miles away. It is, we are told, a "revolving dioptric lens of the first order, with mirrors," which **will without** doubt be intelligible to every reader, be he scientific **or not. It has one** centre lamp **of three** concentric wicks, **and is** among the largest and most powerful lights in the world. It shows a bright flash continuing for six **or** eight seconds, and repeated once every **minute.**

The ascent of the **lofty** tower **is** not difficult, in spite of its height, for after mounting the first twenty-two feet, to the main floor, you find yourself **in a large** and airy room where you can sit and rest as long as you please. Above **that are** twelve flights of stairs and twelve other rooms; thus avoiding the continuous, breathless ascent that **is** so fatiguing. Then **comes the** gallery; but before going **out** we **must climb the** steep and narrow stairs into the light itself. **The whole building is most exquisitely kept,** its polished floors **and** glittering brasses being dainty enough for **my** lady's boudoir. By looking into the **lens, you get a** lovely view of the scene below in miniature. The effect **is like** that of a Claude Lorraine glass.

Civil service **means** something **in** Bermuda. **One** of the three keepers told me he had not left his lonely eyrie for a night in seventeen years, and it was evident he considered himself settled for life. Very proud were the three of their stately and beautiful charge, touching the costly and delicate machinery as tenderly as if it were a sentient being and felt their caressing hands.

But it is the view from the gallery we came to see, and out we go, with a word of caution from the guide as to the wind. We are on the very outermost point of the southwestern coast, and from where we stand we can take in the whole island group, from St. George's to Ireland. What a little spot it is, to be sure! — a mere point in the illimitable waste of waters that stretch away to the horizon on every side. The little Isle of Wight is eight times as large. But the view is magnificent beyond description. The coloring, the exquisite, ethereal softness of the changeful tints of sea and sky and purple reefs fading to palest amethyst, while blending with it all is a glow and fire like the light in the heart of a diamond, — this is something that cannot be put into words. To the right and to the left stretch the larger islands, with their fair green shores. Before us lies the Great Sound, studded with fairy islets, each flooded with a mystic glory, beyond which the eye seeks the far horizon. Below us, at our very feet, are "The Sickle" and "The Spectacles" islands, so named from their shape. White houses, half buried in foliage, dot the landscape from one extremity to the other. In short, it is worth the half of one's kingdom to stand for just half an hour, of a clear afternoon, on the lighthouse tower at Gibbs's Hill.

How long we stood there I will not undertake to say. We were very silent. It was not a thing to chatter about. But at length I ventured on a commonplace.

"Nemo," I said, "we have made a mistake."

He looked at me anxiously, disentangling my long veil that the wind had wound about his arm. "In coming up here? Was it too much for you? Dear me, I'm sorry! But it will be easier going down."

"No, no," I said; "it is not that at all. Our mistake was in not coming earlier. One should come here the very first thing, — to get the lay of the land, if for no other reason. It is better than studying a dozen maps."

X.

"WHAT if I were to go to Chubb's Cut to-day, Lady Mither?" said Nemo, one morning as he came in from breakfast. "What would you do with yourself? For it is quite too hard a trip for you."

"'Chubb's Cut'!" I repeated. "What and where may that be?"

"Pilot Scott can answer that question better than I; but it is one of the outermost of the outer reefs. Two or three of us have thought of going out. We should take the Moondyne to Boaz, hire Pilot Scott and his boat for eighteen shillings, take our lunch, and make a day of it. But what would you do, meanwhile?"

"Never mind me," I answered. "I shall write three letters. I shall mend my dress. I shall fill these vases with the pomegranate flowers you brought me from Peniston's yesterday, adding some scarlet heath and two white lilies. Perhaps I shall read a chapter in Mrs. Child's "Life and Letters." Then I shall put on my bonnet and go in search of the amber you wot of, and if my money holds out I shall buy me a cross and a rosary. After lunch I shall ask Saint Catharine to go rowing with me — and " —

" Hold, hold ! that 's enough ! and I think I may leave you with a clear conscience," cried Nemo, as he strode off, laughing.

I carried out my programme to the letter. After a good deal of trouble, I found the place where I had heard there was some fine amber, and it held me fascinated for an hour.

Where does amber get its strange poetic charm ? — a charm of which even its prosaic association with croup cannot rob it? The cyclopædia may go on telling us it is a " fossilized vegetable gum" till doomsday ; but who in his inmost heart believes it ? It is liquid light crystallized. These clear, transparent drops can own no lower origin.

Here in this queer place — a room connected with a common grocery — I found among numberless strings of cheap amber some necklaces and bracelets of rare beauty; clear, translucent orbs that did indeed "answer to the sun."

> " Oh, liquidly the sunlight filters through
>   These shining spheres of warm translucent gold,
>   Changing to drops of rich and wondrous hue,
>   Like precious wine of vintage rare and old."

I bought a necklace, to be worn some day by one whose rich, dark beauty will adorn it : —

"An amulet, not made of gems or gold,
  But drops of light imprisoned from above.
Gold were too heavy, gems too hard and cold;
  And only amber suits the soul of love!"

That evening I bedecked myself with these spoils, not of war, but of research. With an apologetic "Allow me," a lady touched the cross lightly. "This tells its own story," she said. "You found it in Rome?"

"No," I answered; "I found it here, this morning, in a grocery not far from the Bishop's lodge. Rome is everywhere, if one only looks for it."

After lunch Saint Catharine and I went down to the dock, where we speedily found a boat and a stalwart oarsman. He looked to me for orders as he took up his oars.

"Round White's Island first, that we may pay our respects to the Lady of the Prow."

The man looked bewildered for a moment; then a slow smile crept over his dark face.

"You want to go by the old hulk, lady? Is that it?"

"Yes,— the one with the white figure-head."

Very soon we were under the bows of a once magnificent ship,— now a blackened hulk,— looking up at the grand white figure of a woman with strong, impassive face and steadfast eyes that peered out over the deep with earnest, questioning gaze. What had they not seen, those eyes? What storms had she not breasted, what perils had she not encountered, still with that calm, unshrinking front? She was strength, courage, and faith personified."

"'Ora pro nobis, 't is nightfall on the sea,'" we chanted under our breath; and then we glided away, past Fairyland, with its wooded knolls and shady retreats, to Magazine Island. Here great quantities of ammunition are stored, and powder enough to blow up the whole island range. The place is strictly guarded; and by day and by night an armed sentry paces back and forth on the path from the little dock to the magazine or storehouse, peering into the barred entrance to the latter at every turn.

A number of marines were lazily sunning themselves on the rocks. As we rowed around the island, they rose and followed us, keeping us constantly in sight, — whether from mere curiosity, or because it was their duty to keep an eye on all strangers, is more than I can say.

"Can you row into the caves, do you think?" asked Saint Catharine, smiling sweetly.

"Unless it is too near low tide, lady," replied our dark gondolier; and in a moment we were in a low, broad cave, hung with rude stalactites and dripping with moisture.

These caves are to be found all along the coasts, and seem to have been formed —

But I will not attempt to say how, or by what, — unless it may be by the force of the advancing and receding waves washing away the sand and débris, and leaving the hardened coral rock. It would take a geologist — which I am not — to account for them scientifically.

But they are very curious and interesting, full of strange growths and marine formations. Here the sea-anemones cling to the rocks and shrink like the leaves of the sensitive plant if you do but touch them. As large as your hat at one moment, and gorgeous in pink and gold, at the approach of a cane or parasol they will collapse into utter nothingness, and withdraw wholly out of sight in the crevices of the rocks. Here are curious creatures called "suck-rocks" by the boatmen, — a very aristocrat of a shellfish that lives in a lovely boat, daintily curved and jointed, soft ashen gray on the outside and lined with blue satin.

Here, too, perhaps, a Portuguese man-of-war will sail defiantly near you. Little cares he for soldiers or marines, arsenals or ammunition!

We passed negro fishermen with seines, and paused to watch them as they drew in their nets, filled with the scaly spoil.

There was just motion enough to make the

boat dance; the sun was veiled by light, fleecy clouds; the heat was tempered by the gentle breeze.

"Take us out beyond Spanish Point," I said, "where the surf is dashing over the reefs; and then land us at the point."

How lovely it all was! Do you remember it, sweet Saint Catharine, of the dove-like eyes? We strayed about on the shining beach; we climbed the rocks, and, sitting in a sheltered nook, our eyes wandered far across the blue and sparkling bay to the green shores of Somerset and Boaz, picturesque with arched bridges and peaceful as a dream, — then on to Ireland Island, with its forts, its many masts, and all the stir of active live. It is the only busy place in all Bermuda.

We lay on the soft, warm sand, and picked up myriads of shells, — such tiny, frail, softly-tinted things that we could but pity them as we thought of their long buffetings with wind and wave. We repeated, as the small breakers chased each other up the beach, Helen Ludlow's poem of "The Little White Beggars" that begged "for the shells and the seaweed and sand;" and finally, after a long afternoon of pure delight, we got into our boat again, and were rowed slowly homeward in the sunset glow.

Saint Catharine had been in Bermuda much longer than I, and felt herself quite an old resident. "What is that?" I asked, pointing to a low monument gleaming on a lonely point of rock that projected into the sea. "I am sure it has a story."

"A pathetic one," she answered. "Years ago the regiments stationed here were decimated by some terrible epidemic, — yellow fever, I believe. That stone was erected by the survivors in memory of their lost comrades."

"Poor fellows!" I said, as we drifted by. "Do they have yellow fever here? I did not know it. Let's see — when does the next steamer sail?"

"You need not be in haste to get away. There has n't been a case in nineteen years, I am told. But the islands have been ravaged several times by that, or something else."

We floated on down the harbor towards Hamilton, the shores becoming more thickly settled as we neared the quaint white town.

"Do you see that tall cedar, in front of that long, jalousied, and balconied house?" asked Saint Catharine. "That, too, has a story. It is the custom here to plant, if one may use the expression, a little cedar-tree in the frosting of the bride's-cake. The diminutive thing is carefully removed after the cake meets its legitimate fate, and replanted near the dwelling of the wedded lovers. Fifty years or so ago, two little trees decorated a certain bride's-cake. Both were planted afterwards, and they grew side by side for half a century. Not long ago the bride of that ancient wedding died, and one of the trees fell, too. From its fragrant wood her coffin was made. The other waits its turn."

We scarcely heard the dip of the oars, so softly and silently we floated onward. "Come to think of it," I said, at last, "this must be a queer place for a bridal tour. How do they manage it? Do the Hamiltonians go to St. George, and the St. Georgians return the compliment by going to Hamilton?"

"I don't know," she answered, laughing. "One might put up a tent on one of these lovely, uninhabited islands, and so live in sweet seclusion. But have n't you seen the rose-wreathed 'Honeymoon Cottage,' near Fairyland? Perhaps that solves the mystery. A bridal couple are keeping house for a month or two at the Eagle's Nest just now, I believe."

Nemo and his friends came home at night, full of enthusiasm over Chubb's Cut, for which place they had put out from Mangrove Bay in a little boat of twelve foot keel, with two oarsmen. After putting out to sea for about two miles and a half, a breeze sprang up and the smooth sea took on a ruffle. An hour passed before they caught glimpses of the buoys at the Cut, and met the ocean swell that tossed the little boat gloriously. Bermuda was but a faint cloud in the distance, and around them was immensity. While they ate their lunch, dipping their biscuit in sea-water for a relish, the boat drifted nearly to the "fair-way buoy," as it is called, around which the waves dashed tumultuously, making the float tug fiercely at its chain, and keeping up a strange, metallic "clang! clang!" which could only be compared to the sound of a hoarse and heavy bell, struck under water. And then — the reefs!

I foresaw that night that Chubb's Cut was doomed to my *bête noir*. I shall see the inner reefs with all their marvels of form and color, but what of that? I shall never dare to go out in that little boat; and whatever else I may see or not see, to the end of my days I shall be reminded that I have never seen Chubb's Cut!

Query, why is it Chubb's Cut?

XI.

HAVING done much tramping within a day or two, what if we were to take a drive to-day, — a long one to St. George's? We can go by the North Road, the South Road, or the Middle Road. They are all good. But we will take the North, returning by the South. The comfortable carriage has seats for four; but we look dubiously at the one horse, until we are told that on these hard, smooth roads, hewn out of the solid rock, one horse will do the work of two. It is whispered, also, under the rose, that there are not more than four pairs of horses, or "double teams," in all Bermuda.

So off we go, in the cool, clear morning, bright with sunshine and odorous with flower scents. As we bowl swiftly along, the sea sparkles at our left, as if there were a diamond in the heart of every sapphire wave. Between us and it the slight and graceful tamarisk rises like a pale green mist. The Bermudians call it the "salt cedar." Taste it, and you get the very flavor of the brine. To the right are undulating hills and sleepy valleys, with pretty cottages nestling in their green recesses, and here and there a stately mansion perched far up on some height that commands two ocean views. We pass clumps of cedar and thickets of the fan-leaved palmetto. The curious, club-like paw-paw rises, straight as an arrow, with a tuft of leaves at the top, and fruit, looking not unlike a great green lemon, growing directly from the trunk. The aloe is in bloom, and the Spanish bayonet bristles by the wayside. The drooping purple flower of the banana and its heavy clusters of fruit are in every garden. The banana is as omnipresent as the onion.

Often the road passes for long distances between lofty walls of solid rock, from the crevices of which all lovely growths are springing. They are red with the scarlet of the geranium, aglow with the orange of the lantana, or they are hidden by the purple veil of the wild convolvulus. The dainty sweet-alyssum clings to the rock in great patches, and the little rice plant lays its pink cheek against it lovingly. The prickly-pear clasps its fibrous roots round some rough stone, and stretches out an uncouth arm to ward you off. But, as if to make amends, the loveliest, daintiest ferns smile at you, dancing in the wind, and the delicate maiden's-hair waves its soft fronds caressingly as you go by. Here and everywhere spring the life-plant and the blue stars of the Bermudiana. The orange is not now in fruit, but on many of the lemon-trees the yellow globes are hanging like golden lamps.

A long causeway — a gigantic piece of work, massive and strong enough to defy wind and water for ages — connects St. George's with the mainland. As we approach it a fresh and exquisite picture meets us at every turn, while the views from the causeway itself are surpassingly fine. It is nearly two miles in length, and a revolving bridge gives two wide water passages for boats.

The quaint, picturesque old town, which was founded in 1612, seems to bristle with forts. Indeed, this is true of the whole island range, — the Bermudas being, with the exception of Gibraltar, England's most strongly fortified hold. One not to the manner born cannot help wondering why this infinitesimal bit of land in the midst of mighty seas should require a fort on every exposed point; why there should be batteries and martello towers at every turn, and why red-coats and marines should meet you at every corner. But it must be remembered that this is the rendezvous for the British fleet in all these waters, and here vast quantities of arms and ammunition are stored. England doubtless knows her own business; and it cannot be questioned that her **strong** position here would give her an immense advantage, in case — which **may** God forbid! — of her ever going to war with America. Indeed, **on this** point Godet says, in his history of Bermuda published in London, 1860, "Bermuda, conjointly with Halifax, holds in check the whole Atlantic coast of the United States, upon which nature has bestowed no equivalent for naval purposes; and **also** controls **the** West Indies, the Gulf of Mexico, and the south coasts of the United States. Since the exten**sive government works** at Bermuda have been undertaken, **the** island **is found** more convenient, in conjunction with Halifax, as the seat of naval power, **as it** greatly facilitates the dispatch of ships to **the** West India stations and the American Atlantic coast."

Strangers **are not** allowed inside **the** forts. But **we** can climb the heights, **if** we choose, and see the outside of the show. Or, while we are waiting for dinner to be made ready in the old-fashioned inn facing the square, where the landlord himself **will serve you at** table, carving **the joints** with **his own hand, we** can sit on the **broad** veranda overlooking Castle Harbor, **and try to count** the cannon balls stacked, or **piled,** — whatever the orthodox word may be, — **on the dock of** a little island just opposite us.

Tiring of this we can wander about the narrow streets, with their odd balconied and jalousied houses, and imagine ourselves in the Orient. Or we can go to the Public Garden, and sit under the shade of date-palms one hundred and fifty years old, with a tree called here "The Flaming Star," and having great star-shaped flowers of a fiery red, in front of us; and at our right another, which rejoices in the cognomen of "The Monkey Tree." Why, no mortal can tell, unless it is because no monkey could by any possibility climb it. The massive trunk is thickly set with short, sharp, needle-like thorns.

By what curious law of contrasts was it that under these rustling palm-trees, with strange sounds in our ears and unaccustomed sights before our eyes, Nemo and I sat for an hour and talked, not of the things about us, but of influences that had moulded character in a home hundreds of miles away, of graves beneath the sod and in the deep, of the living that we loved and of the dead that we had not forgotten?

But we rise at last to look about us.

Here, in the ivy-covered wall at the left of the lower gate, — a dark slab in a niche, — is the monument of Sir George Somers, for whom the town was named, and in honor of whom the Bermudas were once known as the Somers Islands. Only his heart is buried here. His body lies in White Church, Dorsetshire, England. In the wall above the old monument is a white marble tablet, erected by Lieutenant-General Lefroy, bearing this inscription:—

>Near this spot
>Was interred, in the year 1610, the Heart of the
>Heroic Admiral,
>SIR GEORGE SOMERS, KT.,
>Who nobly sacrificed his Life
>To carry succor
>To the infant and suffering Plantation,
>Now
>THE STATE OF VIRGINIA.
>To preserve his Name to Future Ages
>Near the scene of his memorable shipwreck of
>1609,
>The Governor and Commander-in-Chief
>Of this Colony for the time being caused this
>tablet to be erected.
>1876.

To us Americans, the most remarkable thing about the tablet was the modesty of Governor Lefroy, who was content, in this inscription that will endure for ages, to be known simply as the "Commander-in-Chief of this Colony for the time being." Certainly there was no blowing of his own trumpet here.

Building's Bay, on the North Shore, is believed to be the spot where, after the shipwreck, the "heroic admiral" built his two cedar ships, the Deliverance and the Patience. The Deliverance was a ship of eighty tons, and the Patience of thirty. There was but one bolt of iron used, and that was in the keel of the Deliverance; and the seams of both vessels were closed with a mixture of lime and oil.

Perhaps this is a fitting time and place to turn our eyes backward for a moment. Bermuda was first discovered in 1522, by Juan Bermudas, when on a voyage from Old Spain to Cuba, with a cargo of hogs. When he caught the distant view of the island, which was all he had, he kindly concluded to leave behind a few of his hogs, that they might take possession of the uninhabited island. But a strong gale sprang up, and drove him away with his ship and his swine. So that was the end of that venture.

In 1543, according to Godet, Ferdinand Camelo took formal possession of Bermuda, and is stated to have cut his name and a rude cross on a rock still known as Spanish Rock, on the south side of the main island. The place remained uninhabited, however, and attracted little or no attention until after the shipwreck here of Sir George Somers. When he sailed for Virginia in his little cedar vessels, on the

10th of May, 1610, he left two men behind to hold possession of the fair islands. He reached his destination in thirteen days; but after a short stay in Jamestown again embarked in the smaller of his small craft, and set sail Bermudaward, arriving there on the 19th of June. Shortly after, he died, overcome by age and the great fatigue of his voyages. The few colonists, disheartened and alarmed, sailed for England with his embalmed body, leaving his heart behind as a legacy to the lonely spot that for a while bore his name.

In the Government House Garden at St. George's there may still be found a mutilated slab of coarse stone, on which is engraved the following epitaph, composed by Governor Nathaniel Butler:—

"In the Yeere 1611,
Noble Sir George Somers went hence to Heaven,
Whose well-tried worth, that held him still imploid,
Gave him the knowledge of the world so wide,
Hence, 't was by Heaven's decree, to this place
He brought new quests and name to mutual grace;
At last his soul and body being to part,
He here bequeathed his entrails and his heart."

England now made serious attempts to colonize Bermuda, and succeeded. But as this is not a history, we need not bother ourselves longer with dates and statistics referring to those faraway days. Bermuda had been regarded as a "prodigious and enchanted place, where no one had ever landed but against his will." How completely the tables were turned can be best shown by giving the title-page of a quaint booklet of perhaps a dozen pages, printed in black letter, which the custodian of the Public Library at Hamilton exhibits with much pride. It bears the imprint "London, 1613," and purports to be Sir George's own account of his shipwreck and deliverance.

"A plain Description of the Bermudas, now called Somers Islands — with the manner of their discoverie, Anno 1609, by the ship-wracke & admirable deliverance of Sir Thomas Gates & Sir George Somers,
Wherein are truly set forth the commodities & profits of that Rich, Pleasant, and Healthful
   Countrie,
         With
An addition, or more ample relation of divers other remarkable matters concerning those Islands since then experienced, lately sent from thence by one of the colonie now there resident.
         Ecclesiastes, 3: 11.
   God made everything beautiful in his time.
            London.
   Printed by W. Stansby for W. Walby.
              1613.

To the Reader.

Good Reader this is the first book published to the world touching Somers Islands; but who shall live to see the last? A more full & exact description of the countrie & narrative of the Nature, site, & commodities, together with a true history of the great deliverance of Sir Thomas Gates & his companie upon them, which was the first discoverer of them, thou mayst surely expect, if God will, to come into thy hands. This short narrative, in the meantime, shall rather prepare thee for it, than prevent thee of it."

Who shall decide when doctors disagree? Even as early as 1613, who discovered Bermuda seems to have been a mooted question. But whoever may have been the ostensible commander of the expedition for the relief of Virginia, there is no doubt that Sir George Somers was its ruling spirit, its real leader; and it is interesting to know that Shakespeare is said to have found the germ of "The Tempest" in this curious little book.

It is but a step from the Public Garden to St. Peter's, the oldest church on the islands. In the walls are many interesting tablets, and the sexton will show you the communion service of massive silver, presented by King William III. in 1684, and a very old baptismal bowl, the gift of some local worthy who has long been dust and ashes. One of the quaintest and most characteristic tablets is in memory of Governor Popple. It is as follows: —

>   Died at Bermuda, November 17th, 1744,
>   in the 46th year of his age,
>   The good Governor
>   ALUZED POPPLE, Esq.
> During the course of his administration which to the inconsolable grief of the inhabitants,
>   continued but six years,
> of the many strangers who resorted hither for their health,
>   The *observant* easily discovered in him,
>   Under the graceful veil of modesty,
>   An understanding & abilities equal
>   To a more important trust.
> The *Gay & Polite* were charmed with the unaffected
>   Elegance and amiable simplicity of his manners,
>   And ALL were chear'd
> By his hospitality and diffusive benevolence which
>   steadily flowed and undisturbed
>   from the heart.
>   To praise according to his Merit
>   The Deceased
>   would be but too sensible a reproach
>   To the living,
> and to enumerate the many rare virtues which shone
>   united on the Governor
>   of that little spot
>   were to tell how many great talents
>   and Excellent Endowments are
>   wanting in some

> Whom the capriciousness of Fortune
> exposes
> In more elevated and conspicuous stations.

Alas for poor human nature! Even in Paradise it cannot raise an altar to its own especial favorite, without casting stones at other folk.

To American eyes, its narrow streets and oddly shaped houses give St. George's a charm that is quite distinctive. York Street is but ten feet wide, and, with its gardens crowded with semi-tropical vegetation, it is like an oriental picture.

XII.

AFTER our early dinner, as there seemed to be ample time to go to St. David's, the only one of the five large islands that is not connected with the others by a bridge, we hired a lame colored man to "row us o'er the ferry." St. George's is "beautiful for situation" as seen from the water, its wooded heights rising tier upon tier, crowned with forts and battlements, and white walls gleaming in the sun. Its aspect is much more foreign and picturesque than that of Hamilton, strongly reminding the traveled visitor of Malta. Indeed, so much is one impressed by its narrow streets and something alien in its atmosphere that he inevitably listens for a foreign tongue, and is surprised at hearing plain English.

After a long pull we reached a landing not far from the lighthouse, whither we hastened. This is by no means as fine an affair as the one at Gibbs's Hill, but from its top we gained a magnificent view of the clustered islands in the harbor, the distant "mainland," the wide, far-sweeping ocean, and the white waves dashing themselves into spray upon the hidden reefs, that are, after all is done, the strongest defenses of Bermuda.

St. David's has comparatively few inhabitants; and of these few it is said there are many who have never dared the perils of the deep, and ventured to cross to the other islands. Talk of the curiosity of women! It is actually true that there are women, born on St. David's island, whose desire to see the world and the ways thereof is so slight that they have never even beheld the glories of St. George or Hamilton.

It was said a few years ago that many of the inhabitants had never seen a horse. A fabulous story is afloat, however, to the effect that now there are two horses on the island — one of which is a donkey.

Time grew short, and we hurried back to the landing, where we found that our lame boatman had engaged another man to lend a hand at the oars. It was well; for as we steered to westward, skirting the narrows, we met the strong ocean swell, that tossed the light boat as if it had been but a soap-bubble. The tide was ebbing, and we would have surely been swept out to sea if the two oarsmen had not pulled for dear life, and with all their united strength. He who knows nothing fears nothing. We laughed at the idea of danger, but learned afterwards that our little adventure had not been without a spicing of the real, true-blue article.

"Do you want to go to Joyce's caves?" asked Nemo, as he handed me into the carriage. "I don't know when we shall have a better chance."

"There's no use making two bites of a cherry," I answered. "Let us see them, by all means. How many are there, if I may ask?"

"Two."

"One will answer for me, thank you. You may do the other while I lie on the grass and meditate. But where is the Walsingham cave, sacred to the memory of Tom Moore? Is n't that somewhere about here?"

"It's on the other side, and we will leave it for another day. Enough is as good as a feast, Lady Mither."

We leave the carriage, and pick our way for some distance through thickets of cedar and oleander, with coffee-trees, bamboos, and lemons interspersed, till we reach the desired haven. It proves by no means a haven of rest, however, for the descent into the caves is rough and precipitous. Yet if you are fond of cavernous depths, it pays. Our guide, an intelligent colored man, who owns the place, lights a bonfire of cedar brush, and the transformation scene begins. The dark, damp, and gloomy cavern stretches away through magnificent distances, and through openings in the walls we catch glimpses of other chambers, of whose splendors we are content to dream. Far above us soars the vaulted roof, hung with stalactites, and glittering as with the light of countless jewels. Below us lies a lake, clear and cold, whereon fairies might launch their airy shallops.

When he who exhibited these wonders found, much to his astonishment, that I was not to be cajoled into entering the second cave, which — as the unseen always is — was far more marvelous than the one I had seen, he beckoned to a boy who was leaning on his hoe in a potato patch hard by, and bade him show the lady the jessamines and the shell-flowers.

The former were the common yellow jessamines of our Southern States. The shell-flower, or shell-plant, as it is called indiscriminately, is very curious as well as beautiful, and to give an adequate description of it in words is not easy. The plant itself is not unlike maize, or indian corn; and the long, drooping flower-cluster which takes the place of the ear is sheathed like that in a pale green husk. This husk opens in due time, revealing row upon row of delicate flowers, each a marvel of loveliness. They are often two inches in length, and are at first simply closed bells, softly tinted in pink and white, like the lining of a sea-shell. Hence the name. But, one by one, they unfold, and lo! your bell is a monk's-hood, gorgeous in gold and crimson. Why do not our florists get hold of it?

On the way home we stopped for a moment at the "Devil's Hole." One moment was quite enough. No rendezvous for gods or fairies this, but a natural fish-pond, through whose rocky basin, set in a huge cavernous chamber, the ocean sends its tide continually. The fish, strange creatures called groupers, with great sluggish bodies and horribly human faces, come crowding up to be fed, and stare at us hungrily with their awful eyes.

The drive home was charming as soft airs, flower-scents, and the sea-breeze could make it. The road was hard and smooth. There was neither dust nor mud, nor noise to annoy one. I leaned back luxuriously among the cushions, wondering for the thousandth time how geraniums and lantanas managed, not only to grow, but to lavish their wealth of color when fastened to the bare rocks by perhaps a single root.

"I can't comprehend it," I said. "It is natural enough for the cacti to live without any visible means of support, but I always supposed the geranium needed bread and butter. Do look at those gate-posts! Driver, stop a moment, please."

We were passing a pretty white cottage, in front of which was a low, curving wall. The stone pillars I had irreverently styled gate-posts were square and high, and each was crowned with a large Turk's-head cactus, in full growth and vigor.

"Well, that's a new idea," said I. "Do you suppose there is a hole in the post, in which the pot is sunken? Nemo, what if you were to get out and see?"

"No need of that, lady," said the driver, showing his white teeth. "There is n't any pot. Turk's-heads, they just grow on the stone."

"Do you mean to say," I remarked, severely, "that those things just sit perched up there on top of those posts, and *grow*, without any earth whatever, the whole year round?"

"That's it, lady. They just set there. That's all," and he drove on.

"What are you smiling at, Lady Mither?" asked Nemo, a moment after.

"To think of all the sentiment I wasted on the hewing out of these roads, when we first came," I answered. "But I suppose it was quite reasonable for us to think them the product of convict labor, cemented by blood and tears. It seemed to me that haggard figures, with bowed heads and hopeless eyes, lurked in every shadow thrown by these massive walls: hardened wretches, no doubt, for the most part, yet with now and then an innocent man among them. Think what his life must have been!"

"But you need not think about it, now that you know the convicts had nothing whatever to do with the roads," said Nemo. "So don't worry your blessed heart over might-have-beens."

"It would be interesting, though, if one had time, to look into the details of convict life. There were nine thousand brought here, first and last, and two thousand of them died. Boaz looks like a very paradise, to-day; but what sighs, and groans, and lamentations for home and kindred, must have gone up from its green shores!"

"Now, Lady Mither, let the convicts be," expostulated Nemo, "and console yourself with those flaming pomegranates. Bermuda is a pretty good place to be exiled to; and the chances are that most of the poor fellows were as well off here as they had ever been elsewhere. Besides, you forget what rascals they undoubtedly were, most of them."

"Do you suppose that made it any easier, — to know it was all their own fault? I don't! But I am glad they are not here now, just or unjust. I wonder what these straight, narrow cross-roads, running for the most part east and west, are? They are hardly wider than a country lane, or footpath. There's one, now."

"That's a 'tribe road,' lady," said the driver.

"And what may that be?"

He shook his head. "I always heard them called so," he said. "I don't just know the reason. There used to be 'tribes' here."

"Districts, or divisions, something after the nature of parishes, I fancy," explained Nemo, "into which, as I have heard, the mainland was divided when the island was first surveyed. Perhaps these 'tribe roads' were boundary lines. But we are almost home. Shall we drive round the harbor and say good-night to your palm-trees?"

How quickly we learn to claim as our own that in which we delight!

There are no more striking objects in all Bermuda than the group of five Royal Palms, brought from Grenada fifty years ago. One needs to stand directly beneath them, and to let the eye follow the straight, columnar shafts as they shoot upward into the clear ether, and lay their fronded heads against the tender blue of the sky, before he can fully take in all their grandeur. There is another fine palm, of the same royal race, at Woodlands.

For variety that evening we were shown a huge specimen of the cuttle-fish, captured that day by a Boston clergyman, who, it was quite evident, had by no means renounced the devil and all his works. One glimpse of the creature, horribly repulsive as it was, was enough to insure the nightmare.

XIII.

ALL the Arabian Nights' tales ever told had paled before Nemo's story of the fairy gardens of the underworld at Chubb's Cut. How, then, could I hope for peace of mind until I had at least beheld the glories of the inner reefs?

For, after all, the chief attraction of Bermuda is in her iridescent waters and what lies beneath them. At nine of the clock, one morning, Williams, a bronze Hercules, low voiced, gentle mannered, a trusty boatman, and an enthusiast in his calling, meets us at the dock, with his water-glasses, nippers, and all else needed for a successful trip to the reefs. But our first objective point is Ireland Island; and to gain time we embark on the Moondyne,—a pleasant party of five, with lunch baskets and the ever-present waterproofs and umbrellas. Towing our row-boat, away we glide down the beautiful sunlit bay, winding our way in and out among the fairy islands of the Great Sound, after a fashion strikingly like the passage through the Thousand Islands of the St. Lawrence. Passing the lovely shores of Somerset and Boaz, which last was formerly the convict station, we get good views of the naval and military hospitals, with their broad balconies and shaded grounds. At Ireland Island is her majesty's dockyard, with forts and batteries, all alive with soldiers, marines, and busy workmen. Several men-of-war, with a multitude of smaller craft, are at anchor in Grassy Bay, and the admiral's ship, the Northampton, is lying in the great floating dock, Bermuda, for repairs. This enormous structure, said to be the largest of its kind in the world, was towed over from England in 1868. To naval, military, and business men this is a most attractive spot, but so much red tape must be untied before one can enter the dockyard that we content ourselves with an outside view, and walk across the island to the cemetery. Here, within sound of the moaning sea and the fierce guns of the forts, all is as peaceful and serene as in any country graveyard in New England. Trees wave, flowers bloom, bright-winged birds flit from palm to cedar, and great masses of the scarlet heath burn in the soft, cool light.

But we are most impressed by the records of sudden and violent deaths; for here we find inscriptions instead of the conventional number. "Killed by a fall from the masthead of H. M. ship Daylight." "Drowned off Spanish

Rock." "Died suddenly, a victim to yellow fever." "Erected by his messmates to the memory of ——, who died at sea." So the inscriptions ran. Many of the epitaphs were curious, but all were to me indescribably pathetic. Here are two or three of them : —

"God's finger touched him, and he slept."

The following I found on an old stone, grammar and all : —

"Its age nor youth, nor wealth cannot withstand
Or shun the power of Death's impartial hand.
Life is a cobweb, be it ere so gay,
And Death the broom that sweeps us all away."

"Sacred to the Memory of
Samuel Gillam,
Late Boatswain's mate of the Ship Belvedere, who was accidentally killed by the sheave of the foremast, on the 17th June, 1836, leaving a widow and four children to lament their loss.

Tho' Boreas' blasts and Neptune's waves,
Have tossed me to and fro,
Yet I at last, by God's decree,
Do harbor here below,
Where at an anchor I do ride
With many of our fleet ;
Once more again I must set sail
My Saviour, Christ, to meet."

Some civilians are buried here, and many little children ; and I came upon a pathetic memorial to a fair young English wife, who followed her soldier husband hither-only to give birth to a little child and die on these far-off shores. But for the most part the sleepers in this beautiful God's acre are strong and stalwart men, cut off in the flower of their days.

We lunch in the delicious shade, with the sea at our feet and a bright-eyed, swift-footed little mulatto boy for our Ganymede. Then we row along the coast and through the narrows to the dockyard harbor, bound for the reefs.

As we round the point there is a sudden gathering of the clans and the swell of martial music. Hundreds of soldiers swarm upon the piers and sailors cling to every masthead. Apparently something exciting is going on. The band strikes up "Home, Sweet Home," and the good ship Humber steams out, with all sails set, bound for England, and crowded from stem to stern. She takes home a regiment whose term of service has expired. A storm of cheers bursts from the comrades they are leaving behind, answered by shouts and hurrahs from the happy fellows on board. They scramble up the tall masts, and far out on the yardarms; they cling to the shrouds, waving their caps and shouting themselves hoarse, as the band plays "The Girl I left Behind Me." One agile fellow stands on the very top of the tallest mast, his figure in bold relief against the blue of the sky. As the ship passes the near buoys "Auld Lang Syne" floats plaintively over the deep, and the men on the dock turn soberly, perhaps sadly, to the monotonous routine of duties.

Williams picks up his oars, and we are soon far out among the reefs. It is so still and clear that a water-glass is scarcely needed. Without its aid we can look far down, down, into the azure and amber depths, so translucent, so pure, that the minutest object is distinctly visible. What marvelous growths, what wonderful creations! Is this a submerged flower-garden? Great sea-fans wave their purple branches, swaying to the swell as pine-boughs sway to the breeze. Magnificent sprays of star-coral — some as fine and delicate as lace-work, and so frail that it would be impossible to remove them from their bed, and some like the strong antlers of some forest monarch — grow upon the sides of the deep sea mountains. Here the shelf-coral hangs from the rocks like an inverted mushroom, delicately wrought, and the rose-coral unfolds like a fairy flower. There lie great brainstones, another variety of coral, with their singular convolutions, side by side with finger-sponges, tall, brown, branching sea-rods, sea-cucumbers, and many another wonder. There are **star-fish, sea-urchins,** and **sea-anemones,** — gorgeous creatures in ashes **of rose** and orange, or in pink and brown with dashes of yellow, and **a** flutter of white ruffles that **unfold** as you gaze, like the opening of a flower-bud. And in and around and about them all glide the blue angel fish, with their **fins** just tipped with gold, yellow canary fish, the zebra-striped sergeant majors, and a ruby-colored fish that gleams in the water like a ray of light.

We gather fans and corals; we exhaust our vocabularies in expressions of delight; and then in the soft glow of sunset, while the shores are bathed in rosy mist, and each little island is an emerald or an amethyst set in silver, and the far lighthouse towers above them all like a watchful sentinel, we half row, half **float, home-**ward with the tide, silent, tired, but **happy.**

Yet two of the party said, "Yes, **this was all** very fine. But if you could only see the reefs at Chubb's Cut!"

XIV.

It rained that night, and in the morning there was a chill north wind, putting a damper upon a pleasant plan of ours. We had meant to take a long, delightful ten-mile drive to Sandys — most of the way by the blue, blue sea — and attend church there. For it was Sunday again. But as it was, we chose to sit with closed door and windows and read Emerson instead. Every five minutes, however, one or the other of us stepped out on the balcony to see if the pennant flying at Mount Langton bore witness that the mail steamer was signaled.

Flags talk in Bermuda after a most bewildering fashion. They give you all kinds of information if you are only quick-witted enough to take it in: when it is church time, and when it is noon; when an unknown ship is in sight; when the mails will close; when they go out, and when they come in; when a boat is wanted at Mount Langton; when there is a vessel on the rocks; when the Pioneer will call at the "Ducking Stool," — whatever that may be, —

and when it will not call. There is no end to the signals; but it would take a lifetime and the patience of Job to master their language.

In the afternoon the sun came out; earth, air, sea, and sky wooed us as entrancingly as ever, and Bermuda was her fair, sweet self again. Out-of-doors was far better than in-doors, and we started out for a purposeless stroll, not caring whither we went. Not far from our lodgings, a path led into a pretty, secluded grove. What better time to explore it?

It developed erelong into something very like a smooth wood-road in Vermont. The air was sweet with the faint odor of the ferns and the aromatic breath of the cedars. Not a sound was to be heard but the low warbling of a bird.

"Are we really in Bermuda?" asked Nemo. "I half believe we are at home, taking a stroll up beyond the Quarter-line. We shall come, pretty soon, to the old oak with the hole in it, where Fred hid my cane last summer."

But we did not, though we passed several unproductive "quarries," that were familiar in name if not in appearance. Instead of the oak we found a grove of palm-trees and a wild growth of orange and lemon trees, and instead of the shy arbutus the drooping bells of the life-plant. The golden-rod was there, lifting its yellow plumes in the April sunshine. How out of place it looked! We longed for tender blue violets instead, or fair, spring-like hepaticas. It made us wonder if one would not tire after a while of perpetual summer-time, — even of roses and lilies and soft sunlit skies, charming as they all were in contrast with the long winter from which we had fled. Beautiful Bermuda can never know what spring is, — the joy of the awakening earth, the miracle of the new creation. She has much that we have not; but she can never have the green splendor of widespreading elms, or oaks, or maples, the glory of autumnal foliage, or the white wonder of the snow.

At last, as we strolled on, we caught a glimpse of the sea, and came out into the road near Mr. Trott's garden, famous for its lilies. There were thousands of the great white chalices, each upheld by its slender shaft of emerald, and "filled to faintness with perfume."

While Nemo went on down to the shore, to reconnoitre, I stopped to speak to a colored woman, who led by the hand a wee atom of a girl, the tiniest creature that ever walked on two feet. She was like a little bronze statuette; only bronzes do not break into soft, dimpling laughter when they are spoken to, nor mantle with pink flushes under their golden browns. As I stooped to bring my tall self a little nearer to her level, she smoothed down her white dress, gave me her mite of a hand, smiling in the friendliest fashion, and informed me that her name was Lily. This sixteen months old baby could hardly be expected to have any behavior, good or bad; but it is true that as a rule the colored children are exceptionally well behaved, and many of them are very pretty.

Nemo reported nothing of special interest farther on. So, turning back, we struck a path that apparently led to our beloved Serpentine, and concluded to venture it. Straiter and steeper grew the way, till it culminated in two or three flights of stone steps, up which we clambered wearily, to find ourselves in a wide expanse of pasture land, and no road in sight.

When, after devious wanderings, we struck the Serpentine, it was at a point a mile from home.

Tired? Well — rather!

"But, for a woman who could n't walk when she came to Bermuda, it seems to me you are doing pretty well, Lady Mither," said Nemo; and I agreed with him, even if it was true that on the morrow the spirit did not move me to herculean tasks.

And so the weeks went on. "Bermuda is

dull, Bermuda is slow," said some one, now and then. "It is so quiet here, and there is nothing going on."

"There is not even anything to dress for," was sometimes said; and it must be confessed this was a trial to Miss Flora MacFlimsey, who remarked dolefully that she had such lovely white dresses, all puffs and laces and embroideries, in her trunk, and it was not warm enough to wear them, whereas at Nassau, etc., etc., etc.

But the days flew too fast for most of us. Whether we walked, or rode, or sailed, or simply sat in sun or shade and vegetated, there was nothing to regret save that the day was drawing near when we must strike our tents and steal away.

One morning Nemo and the Colonel proposed a trip that was quite beyond my powers. "Run away," I said, "and make a long day of it, and a hard one if you please. But the little brunette and I are going to Camp Warwick this afternoon."

We started after lunch.

"We shall strike the military road after a little," said the brunette.

This sounded well; and as it was probable that military roads were far superior to civil roads, I waited the event with much interest, only to find myself on the very worst road I had yet **traversed in** Bermuda. Our objective point was the beach opposite Camp Warwick, — a beach with high, overhanging cliffs jutting out into the sea.

When we left the carriage, to go down to the shore, gleams of scarlet and the flash of bayonets led our eyes to a rock on which were clustered a dozen red-coats and as many musicians, their brass instruments glittering in the sun.

"Something is going on," said my companion. "They are getting ready to fire. Do you dare venture down?"

But just then a young lieutenant approached, with grave salute, and, telling us that target practice was about to begin, begged permission to place us where we could see the firing and yet be out of harm's way.

It is needless to say we stayed not on the order of our going, but followed him with all speed.

"There is nothing new under the sun," I said, after he left us to rejoin his men. "But this is really a novel situation for two New England women. Here we are on this dot of an island in mid-ocean, perched on a coral cliff, and watching the soldiers of Old England as they learn to fight her battles."

"Ping! ping! ping!" went the rifles; and

"Boom! boom! boom!" answered the waves, as they beat upon the rocks below us.

We climbed down to the beach after we had watched the soldiers long enough, — a beautiful white beach, composed entirely of shells and coral ground fine by the action of the waves. I filled my handkerchief with the débris, which had not the slightest intermixture of sand or soil; but not one unbroken shell could we find.

Nemo and the Colonel returned to a late dinner, with reports of a delightful day under Pilot Scott's guidance. He had taken them round Somerset, through Sandys Narrows into the Great Sound, and from thence to Boaz in time to catch the Moondyne on her return trip. This course led them to Daniel's Head, where they found a ruined fortification of two hundred years ago; and to Elie's Harbor, where they landed at Whale Island, and ate their lunch in the lee of the ruined ovens, or boilers, which were formerly used for trying out blubber.

"Did you go to Basset's cave?"

"Certainly," said the Colonel. "What pair of adventurous spirits could go out for a day in Bermuda without entering the bowels of the earth on one pretext or another? But for which reasons I have been unable to discover, few people visit Basset's cave, although it is quite as picturesque and beautiful as the Walsingham, which everybody goes to see."

"You may as well tell us about it," said I, "for I'm not going there, — neither is Saint Catherine. We are not over-fond of underground passages."

"Then why should you hear about them? But Pilot Scott rowed us to the shore, and, led by a little negro boy, we came to a rocky opening in the side of a low hill. Lighting candles, we crept slowly in, clambered down steep pathways which were damp and slippery, and soon came to a little underground lake. Here we set fire to a pile of cedar boughs which our small guide had gathered, and the bright flames lit up the water and the dark recesses of the cave. Stalactites hanging from the ceiling and stalagmites rising from the floor glistened in the unusual light, and the clear emerald water of the little lake — salt sea-water which falls and rises with the tide — seemed to be a great jewel in a setting of coral. It was too slippery to venture further, and when the boughs had all been burned we climbed out into the sunshine again. That was all there was of it. Nothing very dreadful, you perceive; but we did not see so much as the ghost of a water nymph or a peri."

"I don't know a great deal about caves," remarked one of the ladies, "and I have n't been into one of them. But I would like to ask if it is impossible to have a cave without a lake? That same 'little lake' that the Colonel speaks of has figured in every cavern I have heard of yet. Hear this, will you!" and with a laughing glance at a gentleman who was absorbed in a game of whist at a table opposite, she drew a letter from her pocket. "I did n't write it, but it is a description of the Walsingham cave, and it goes to New York by the Oronoco next Thursday. Now see if they are not as much alike as two peas. No, George, go on with your whist," she added, shaking her head at the gentleman, who half rose from his chair. "I can manage this business myself. I'll skip the preliminaries." And she read, —

"The Walsingham caves, which I mentioned above, lie near the quaint white town of St. George's, and are entered from the side of a little hill. The rude stairs, hollowed out of the coral rock, wind about in many directions, and the entrance is very narrow. When the visitor has descended fifteen or twenty feet, however, he finds himself in a room of peculiar beauty. The walls are hung with stalactites, and in the centre of the chamber is a lake of emerald water, which sparkles in the light of blazing cedar boughs, while the drops which fall from the ragged ceiling tinkle musically upon the rocks and water below. A cool, delicious air fills the cave, and the silence of the place is so intense that the quiet groves seem filled with humming noises when one climbs to the face of the earth again; and the sunshine is marvelously bright, even in the shade of the ancient calabash which guards the forbidding entrance."

"There it is, you see," she went on, laughingly, as she refolded the letter and slipped it into its envelope: "little hill, little lake, emerald water, cedar boughs, and all. They're all alike, and why you gentlemen find them so interesting that you must needs creep — no, crawl — into every one of them passes my comprehension. I'd rather have one square yard of her blue sky than all the subterranean depths in Bermuda."

"Which is conclusive," retorted the courteous Colonel, bowing serenely; "especially when you acknowledge that you have not seen one of these same depths. I maintain that the descriptions are not alike, inasmuch as I said nothing whatever about 'delicious air,' 'intense silence,' 'tinkling drops,' nor 'ancient calabashes.' They were not to be found in *my* cave — unless it may have been the silence."

XV.

It would be impossible to tell of all the pleasant excursions that gave light and color to our Bermudian days. One morning we drove to Tucker's Town, — about seven miles, — and there hired a whale-boat and three stout oarsmen for the day, that we might explore Castle Harbor and its surroundings. With a single square-sail set, we bounded over the light waves toward Castle Island, but after beating about for a little while made a landing at the extreme point of the mainland, that the gentlemen might visit a cave called the Queen's White Hall. The Point is uninhabited, and never a sound could be heard except the husky murmur of the slow waves as they breasted the rocks or rolled in upon the seaward beach.

The ladies, meanwhile, climbed the high cliffs, to watch the breakers afar off and wait for their escorts. Suddenly there was a rush, a whirr of wings, laughter, and a call to us, — and down we went.

The lighting of a bit of magnesium wire had disclosed a boatswain bird on its nest.

Blinded by the sudden glare, it had given one fearful cry ere it was caught and brought out for our inspection. The boatswain is a beautiful white creature, of the gull family, with two long feathers in its tail, by means of which it is popularly supposed to steer its flight; hence the name. When we let it go, it flew far out to sea. But we were scarcely in the boat again when we saw it circling and wheeling far above our heads, only waiting till we strange intruders should be gone before returning to its nest.

"Now you are down here, ladies," said the Colonel, "you ought surely to enter Her Majesty's White Hall. You'll never have another chance; and this is really a cavern without a lake."

How we crept in through the narrow entrance I shall never try to tell. But the passage grew wider as we followed the winding way, and when our eyes became accustomed to the darkness we could see that the floor was hard white sand, and that small stalactites hung from the narrow roof above us. It is not a large cave, but is weird and strange. Though we were less than fifty feet from the door the waves were no longer heard. How still it was! — so still that our footfalls on the smooth sand seemed loud and harsh.

Having set sail again, we made for Castle

Island. Steep stairs cut in the rocks led us to a broad plateau bordered by ruined fortifications, massive structures which were built early in the seventeenth century, when the Spanish buccaneers made constant raids upon Bermuda. In fact, the pirates once held Castle Island, and we walked over the paths their feet had worn nearly three hundred years ago. Afterwards the castle was for a time the seat of government. The massive walls of fort and castle, full ten feet thick, seem as if they might stand forever.

Climbing up into one of the deep embrasures, with the lonely sea before me and the silent court behind, I tried to imagine the scene as it was when gay with red-coats and gold-laced officers, with their powdered wigs, their queues, their queer cocked hats, and all the pomp and pageantry of glorious war. Far down on the beach below me lay a rusty cannon, half buried in the sand. Doubtless from the very spot where I stood it had belched forth its thunders at the approaching pirate fleets.

We lunched in the gray old court, sitting on a low stone seat whereon, it was easy to believe, many a brave soldier and many a fair lady had whispered sweet secrets, long ago. Names were carved in the rocks and on the walls, the numbers of many regiments — some famous in English annals — appearing over and over again. The remains of the old ovens were still there, and chimneys blackened by the smoke of fires so long gone out.

In the old Government House there is a hall, floorless and windowless now, where many a Bermuda girl danced and was made love to by the gay gallants of other days. For Bermuda has always been gay, — gayer, they say, in the past than it is now. So long ago as when our Puritan fathers were struggling with cold, with savages, and with all the hardships and privations of early New England life, Bermuda was sitting in the sun and smiling as serenely as to-day. The traditions there are not of spinning and weaving, of hard-won comforts, of serious endeavor, of Indian fights and cruel massacres, but of gay *fêtes* and brilliant masquerades, of happy competence and careless ease. The old ladies of to-day show you the fine dresses, the laces and ornaments, that their great-grandmothers wore when they, the great-grandmothers, were young.

Setting sail again, we swept through the great harbor, passing Nonsuch and Cooper islands and rounding St. David's Head, a magnificent promontory, against which the sea beat itself to foam. The wind was high; we were in the open sea, and the boat was tossed like a feather by the great waves that came rolling in from beyond the reefs. The headlands of St. David's are precipitous cliffs, with deep bays and curious indented caves. One of them is called Cupid's Oven, — a most maladroit name, for the little god would be frightened out of his wits by the mere sight of the dark, uncanny hole. Elsewhere a door is cut in the high ocean wall. Does it lead down to Hades?

We entered the narrows just beyond the island, and the oarsmen, the sail being lowered, pulled along the coast to St. George's. Here our carriages were in waiting, and we drove home by the way of Moore's Calabash Tree, in a dark, secluded glen. The poet, it is said, was wont to sit here and sing of the charms of Bermudian girls.

A gay deceiver he; for while writing love-songs to "Nea," the "Rose of the Isles," and praising her beauty and her grace, he writes to his mother thus: —

"These little Bermuda islands form certainly one of the prettiest and most romantic spots that I could ever have imagined, and the descriptions which represent it as a place of fairy enchantment are very little beyond the truth. From my window, now as I write, I can see five or six different islands, the *most* distant not a mile from the others. They are covered with cedar groves, through the vistas of which you catch a few pretty white houses, which my practical shortsightedness always transforms into temples; and I often expect to see nymphs and graces come tripping from them, when to my great disappointment I find that a few miserable negroes are all the 'bloomy flush of life' it has to boast of. Indeed, you must not be surprised, dear mother, if I fall in love with the first pretty face I see on my return home; for certainly the human face divine has degenerated wonderfully in these countries, and if I were a painter and wished to preserve my ideas of beauty immaculate, I would not suffer the brightest belle of Bermuda to be my housemaid."

Why will people preserve their old letters?

Moore was appointed "Registrar to the Admiralty in Bermuda" in 1803. He came to the islands that same year, but returned in 1804, leaving a deputy to discharge the duties of the office. In relation to this, he writes to the same correspondent: —

... "I shall tell you at once that it is not worth my while to remain here. . . . I acquit those who persuaded me to come. They did not know about the situation. Am not sorry I came. The appointment is respectable, and a valuable step to future preferment. **The Bermuda court has** few causes referred to it, and even a Spanish war would not make my income by any means worth staying for. However, there are **two** American ships for trial. I have been bettered by acquiring knowledge of men and affairs, and by roughing it. Hope you and 'darling father' won't feel disappointed at the damp our expectations have experienced. . . . How I shall enjoy dear Katie's playing when I return! The jingle they make here upon things **they** call piano-fortes is, oh! insupportable. . . . Your own, own, affectionate **T. M.**"

His next letter, dated January 24, 1804, is sent by way of the West Indies, and announces that he expects to sail for England in May or **June.** It reiterates his dislike of the place. "It is now nearly twelve o'clock. I have just returned from a grand turtle feast, and am full **of** calipash and madeira."

Under date of February 11, he complains that he had not heard from home, by letter or newspaper, for five months, and still harps upon the poor position and the Spanish war. But, he adds, "It is impossible to be ill in such a climate. **Roses** are in full bloom here now, and my favorite green peas smoke every day upon the table. . . . I have been very fortu**nate here** (as indeed Providence seems to please I should be everywhere) in conciliating friendship and interesting those around me in my welfare. The admiral, Sir Andrew Mitchell, has insisted upon my making his table my own during my stay here, and has promised to take me in his ship to America for the purpose of getting a passage to England, — there being no direct conveyance from this corner thither. . . . They threaten me here with impeachment, as being in a fair way to make bankrupts of the whole island. There has been nothing but gayety since I came, and there was never such a furor of dissipation known in the town of St. George's before. The music parties did not keep long up, because they found they were obliged to trust to me for their whole orchestra; but the dances have been innumerable, and still continue with great spirit indeed. The women dance in general extremely well, though, like Dogberry's 'writing and reading,' it comes by nature to them, for they never have any instruction except when some flying dancing-master, by the kindness of fortune, happens to be wrecked and driven ashore on the island. Poor things! I have real pity for them."

Dancing, feasting, making love to the girls for whom he had such pity, bewailing his fate, and talking about a war with Spain, which he seems to have desired above all things, varied by fits of enthusiasm over the wonderful coloring of the Bermudian seas, his days went on, until he writes from New York under date of May 7, 1804: —

"Here I am after a passage of nine days from Bermuda, never better, and novelty keeps me in bustle. Such a place! such a people! Barren and secluded as poor Bermuda is, I think it a Paradise to any spot in America I have ever seen."

The mercurial poet seems to have been rather hard to suit.

To go back for one moment to our day's excursion. In the long, and for our men hard, trip, we did not hear from them one loud word, much less an oath. The captain, a handsome young negro, gave his orders by a look, a word, a sign, and was obeyed as quietly.

XVI.

Her Majesty does not provide for her representatives in Bermuda very luxurious or elegant mansions. Neither Mount Langton, the Government House as it is called, nor Clarance Hill, the Admiralty House, are fine buildings. Indeed, they are quite the opposite. But both places are beautifully situated, with fine grounds and extensive gardens; and what does it matter if the house be fine or otherwise, when one lives out-of-doors? The *bougainvillea* or *bourganvillier* — the name of the vine was spelled for me in both ways by those who were supposed to know how — that covers the thirty-foot wall of the long avenue leading to the Government House with a glory of crimson bloom such as no words can paint is enough in itself to compensate for many lacks in drawing-room and boudoir.

Invitations came one day. "Mrs. Gallway — At home — Saturday, April 21, from three to six." To this were added the cabalistic words "Lawn Tennis."

Would we go? Of course we would, if only

for the sake of having another look at that vine, and at the large lemon-tree whose golden lamps were a perpetual marvel.

A somewhat stately "gentleman in black" awaited us at the portal of the low, rambling yellow house that rejoices in the name of Mount Langton, took our cards, and piloted us through the mazes of the grounds to the great lawn, where Mrs. Gallway and her daughters were "receiving." A fine regimental band discoursed eloquent music from a wooded hill at our left. Below us were the tennis courts, where the gay combatants were already at war. Clumps of palms, cedars, and pride-of-India trees gave an abundance of pleasant shade; and beneath were tables spread with dainty fare and gay with fruits and flowers, for such as did not care to go to the house for afternoon tea. Mrs. Gallway, a pale little lady in black, with a gentle, refined face, received her guests with simple courtesy; but being in frail health she soon disappeared, leaving them to their own devices.

It was a pretty sight, the uniforms of the officers, the black coats of the civilians, and the light dresses of the ladies mingling in happy contrast, while the swift-footed tennis players kept up a changeful kaleidoscopic stir of light and color. Rustic seats in abundance gave opportunity for rest and pleasant chattings.

"There are many pretty girls in this little island," I remarked to a Bermudian lady; my eye wandering from one graceful group to another, and my mind reverting to Tom Moore's disparaging judgment. But she answered, with a smile, —

"Indeed, all the really pretty girls you see here are Americans. We lose our good looks very young. We lose our complexions. But the American girls are beautiful, and they have such charming manners."

I bowed my acknowledgments for this compliment to my young countrywomen.

"But why is it?" I asked, replying to what she had said of her own. "Not that I admit the truth of your assertion; but allowing that it is true, how do you explain it?"

"In many ways," she answered. "It is owing to the saltness of the air, no doubt, and to the sun, and the white roads. Then we live on the water. We are at sea always in Bermuda; and you know how even a voyage across the Atlantic darkens one. Our voyage lasts forever."

"I have discovered one thing," I said, glancing at a group of young girls whose rebellious tresses were flying in the wind, and tucking a straightened lock of my own behind my veil. "Whatever else women can do in Bermuda, they can't keep their hair in crimp. But they can wear fresh roses all the year round, which is far better."

Just then the rising wind soughed and sighed through the palms and cedars, increasing in strength until we older folk were fain to seek the shelter of the broad verandas, and refresh ourselves with tea and sponge cakes. Who won the games that day I never knew.

Not long after this, half a dozen persons, three of whom at least were not in a very hilarious mood, were waiting on the dock with wraps and waterproofs. A sail-boat was making its swift way towards them.

"Is everything packed?" asked one of the party. "Are you all ready?"

"Everything," was the answer, — "shells, corals, sea-fans, palmetto work, cedar boxes, charcoal sketches, and all. We are ready for the flitting, having determined long ago that sink or swim, survive or perish, we would leave this afternoon free for our last sail. But here comes the boat. This is your waterproof, Hetty. Careful now, Miss Alice. There you are! Mrs. Blank, you will need your sun umbrella. Hold on a minute, skipper, till I get that basket."

"This is a curious arrangement," said Nemo, looking about him critically. "We have been in row-boats, whale-boats, flat-boats, ferry-boats, open yachts, and steam-tugs, to say nothing of steam-ships. But, Lady Mither, this is certainly the very first time that you and I ever went to sea in a tub."

"Like the three wise men of Gotham," quoth I. "Only their tub was a bowl. But do you mean to say I have got to get into that — I don't know what to call it — that square orifice in the middle?"

"Certainly, Lady Mither. That's the cabin. The thing is what they call 'flush-decked,' and it has no gunwale. You can sit on the roof if you please, but as there is a good stiff wind you'll be more comfortable down here."

He gave me his hand, and I descended a flight of steep steps into the little cabin. The six — no, eight — of us filled it completely; and as we stood in a clustered group, the heads only, of the shorter ones, the heads and shoulders of the taller, were above board. We were literally in a deep tub with sails. But the strange creature fairly flew down the bay, rushing through the tortuous channels and avoiding the hidden reefs as if by the help of magic.

Accidents, it is said, occur very rarely in these waters, notwithstanding the fact that both the yachts and the little open boats called "dingeys" carry an enormous amount of canvas. Every Bermudian boy learns to manage a boat as he learns to walk or to whistle. It "comes by nature;" and by the time he is fairly into trousers he is also into something that can float. The Royal Bermuda Yacht Club and an Amateur Boating Club are very popular, and their periodic races make gala days for the whole island. The "event of the year" is the race for the Duke of Edinburgh's "cup." On one of these occasions a yacht of under five tons, and of only sixteen feet keel, carried a stretch of canvas measuring fifty-eight and a half feet from side to side; and a dingey of ten feet keel, when running before the wind, carried by actual measurement a spread of forty-two feet.

I am too entirely a landswoman to know whether these figures are remarkable or not. But as the men seemed to think them so, I give them for what they are worth.

On we flew for miles, winding in and out among the islands of the Great Sound. But neither the swift, inspiring motion nor the wine-like air drove the unwonted shadow from certain faces.

"Homesick, already?" I said to one doleful individual.

"Yes, I am," he answered, bluntly. "That's the worst of coming to Bermuda, — that one must go away again. Look at that water! Did you ever see anything like it? Throw all the sapphires and rubies and emeralds and amethysts in the world into one vast crucible, and melt them up, and you might get something that would approach it — at a distance."

"Yes, but you would need to add the yellow topaz and the flash of diamonds, also," I said.

"And showers of pearls, like hoar-frost, and broken rainbows without number. One can't put it into words! Why should we try?"

"Yet through all the shifting play of color, how the pure blue predominates! Blue above, and blue below. It is as if we were living in the heart of a sapphire."

Does this seem like exaggeration?

But it is not. One learns to be chary in the use of adjectives, to beware of telling the whole truth, lest he should seem to color the word picture too warmly. Blue! blue! blue! If the printer whose fate it is to put these sheets in type finds his font exhausted of b's, and l's, and u's, and e's, it is not my fault, but the fault of Bermudian seas and skies.

"How did you people happen to come here?" I asked that evening, addressing one member of a party who had traveled very widely. "Was it because Bermuda happened to be the only spot on the habitable globe untrodden by your adventurous feet?"

"Not exactly," he answered, laughing. "We have not been quite everywhere, yet. But one thing we are all agreed upon: nowhere have we found within the compass of nineteen square miles so much that was novel, beautiful, and interesting, with such air and such sunshine and such peace, as we have found just here."

XVII.

ONE can't get lost in Bermuda. Walk where you will, or drive, if you dare, — for Bermudians turn to the left, and Americans are apt to come to grief, — you will be sure to come out in sight of some well-known landmark. Never to be forgotten is one bright afternoon, when two of us drove all by ourselves to Knapton Hill and Spanish Rock.

Tethering our horse to a convenient tree, we walked to the latter through a pleasant cedar grove on the hillside, intersected by winding paths that apparently had no object in life save to wander at their own sweet will. Birds were singing, wild flowers blooming at our feet; we were shut in from all sight or sound of the sea, and again we were forcibly reminded of our northland, and the evergreen hills so far away.

But presently we came out by a brackish sort of pond, that was very unlike our clear, cold, sparkling, mountain lakes. Its sandy shores were completely riddled with crab-holes. Beyond it were bold, ragged rocks and beetling crags, over and round which we made our difficult way, to be repaid by the wildest and grandest sea-view in Bermuda.

From the far horizon the great, strong waves came sweeping in impetuously, a mighty host, dashing madly against the resistless rocky barrier that barred their way, and in impotent rage and dying passion leaping wildly as to mid-heaven.

Just so, with just such frantic fury, did they storm and shout when, centuries ago, a Spanish ship went down before them, and Ferdinand Camelo, escaping as by a miracle, carved his name and a rude cross, with the date 1543, upon this "Spanish Rock."

Sacred, too, is the memory of another day, when, in the same delightfully independent fashion, we went to Spanish Point (which, by the way, must not be confounded with Spanish Rock, one being on the North Shore and the other on the South), intending to spend an hour upon the shining beach. But when we got there it was flood tide, and the whole broad expanse was under water.

So turning back, we stopped for a while to hold a laughing interview with the funniest little donkey in the world, a diminutive creature tethered by the roadside, that tugged at its rope in a frantic effort to approach us, all the while braying terrifically. How so small a beast could make so great a noise was past all comprehension. After vain attempts to console him with comfits of fresh grass and lovely yellow thistles, we left him to his lonely lot, and, having reached a cross-road just in front of Admiralty House, crossed the island to the North Shore.

The water was so marvelously clear that from cliffs forty feet above the sea we could count the shells and pebbles lying twenty feet beneath it.

As we drove slowly along, feeling it was joy enough just to be alive in that soft, enchanted air, and within sight of the far-stretching sea, that was as tranquil and placid that day as if it had never so much as dreamed of luring the sons of men to destruction, an unwonted commotion on the rocks below us brought us to a standstill. What was going on?

England was on the alert, as usual, and had discovered an unprotected point in her domains. Another cannon was to be planted on this coast instanter. But judging from the fuss that was made in unloading it, and from the delays and the unhandiness of the procedures, in spite of the frantic excitement of a fat man, who had doffed his red coat and was flying about in his shirt-sleeves, the feat seemed likely to be accomplished in Bermudian rather than English fashion.

"If we come this way again in the course of a year or two, that weapon of war will be in place," said Nemo. "But suppose we go on now."

By and by we turned off into a road that was new to us, leading up a hill, and lined with oleanders, pink, white, and crimson, as large as good-sized apple-trees. We did not know where it led, nor did we care. But we came out at last near the old church in Devonshire, an ivy-covered ruin. Having been warned that the roof might fall, we did not go inside, but through the broken windows we saw the crumbling walls, from which the precious tablets had been removed, the dilapidated pews, and the high pulpit with antique hangings, faded and hoary. In one of the aisles was stowed away a ghastly hearse and a tottering bier, on which, no doubt, many generations of the dead who were sleeping so soundly, hard by, had been borne to their last rest. I turned away with a shudder.

But without, how sweet and still it was! It was late afternoon. Not a sound reached us, not even the lapsing of the waves. Only now and then a lone bird twittered softly, or the winds sighed in the palm-trees. Great gray tombs lay all around, like huge sarcophagi, and stretched far up the hill, weird and sombre in the light of dying day. Perhaps it was against the rules, — I don't know, — but with a great lump in my throat, and a tender thought of the little unknown sleeper, I picked a rose from a bush that was heaping a child's grave with its fragrant petals. If it was a sin, I here make full confession, and crave absolution from the baby's mother! Rose geraniums grew wild in great profusion, making the air sweet with their strong perfume. It is called in Bermuda the "graveyard geranium," and I was told that pillows for coffined heads are filled with the fragrant leaves. An immense but dying cedar — the oldest on the islands — stands near the church, and was formerly used as a bell-cote. The trunk is hollow, and inside it two vigorous young trees are growing.

More than one rainy morning we spent in the public library, established in 1839, poring over curious old books and quaint records; but we were especially interested in the files of the "Royal Gazette" in bound volumes, running back precisely a hundred years. Turning over the yellow leaves one day, I came across, under the head of "Latest American News," a thrilling account of the difficulties between the New Yorkers and the Green Mountain boys, and of a conflict at Brattleboro, under **Colonel** Wait. The "Royal Gazette" **still** lives, a quaint little sheet which looks like **a** fac-simile of an American paper of **the last** century. You can buy it for a sixpence, and read it through, advertisements and all, in twenty minutes.

There are no springs in Bermuda, and the great water-tanks are conspicuous objects everywhere. Built of heavy stone, cool, dark, and entered solely by a door in the side which admits the bucket, the water they contain is limpid and delicious. Every householder is compelled by **law** to **have a** tank, and to keep it in good repair.

Another thing that attracts attention is the animals tethered here, there, **and** everywhere. You see donkeys, goats, cows, even cats, hens, and turkeys, — these last drooping sulkily, or swelling with outraged dignity, — confined by the inevitable tether. Noticing the strange manœuvres of a hen in an inclosure near the road, I stopped to investigate, and discovered that **she was tied by** a cord two yards long to another hen. Their gyrations and flutterings were attempts to **walk** in opposite directions, — a pair of unaccommodating Siamese twins.

XVIII.

But time would fail to tell of all that filled our Bermudian days with a satisfying, restful delight: of trips on the Moondyne; of moonlit walks to Hungry Bay, when the spray was hoar-frost and the waves were rippled silver; of Saturday mornings at Prospect, to see the fine drill of the Royal Irish Rifles; of amateur theatricals given by the officers and their wives in the rickety old theatre; of pleasant hours in Bermudian homes; of kindly greetings and warm hand-clasps. Shall I ever forget a certain "afternoon tea," where we were served in the shaded balcony by the five fair daughters of the house, while the happy and handsome mother smiled serenely, and took her ease with the rest of us; or a morning in a quaint old place at Point Shear, where a lovely lady and the dearest of little boys opened their hearts as well as their home to their stranger guest, giving her some never-to-be-forgotten glimpses of the treasures in each? Can I ever forget the little Abacado pear-tree, and the bath-house, like a fairy's grotto, and the shells and corals lavished upon me with such sweet persuasion, or lose the fragrance of the roses I bore away with me? They faded long ago, but their perfume lives on. And shall I ever cease to remember the mangroves, looking for all the world like tipsy bacchanalians, that in some way always reminded me of Saxe Holm's story of the "One-Legged Dancers"?

A few last words as to the climate. It is somewhat capricious, but is never really cold. Bermuda has no frosts. Yet during seven weeks, beginning in March and ending in May, we were in no need of thin summer clothing. The mercury in winter seldom falls below 60°. In the height of summer it is seldom above 85°, and there is always the breeze from the sea. When it blows from the southwest, Bermudians stay within doors, and remain quiet till it changes. Tropical plants thrive, not because it is hotter than with us in summer, but because they are never winter-killed.

Bermuda is *not* the place for consumptives. But for the overworked and weary, for those who need rest and recreation and quiet amusement, for those who love the beauty of sea and sky better than noisy crowds and fashionable display, and can dispense with some accustomed conveniences for the sake of what they may gain in other ways, it is truly a paradise.

This paradise has one great advantage over other paradises, — an advantage it must retain for many years, if not forever. Its very inaccessibility, being reached only, during the greater part of the year, by a semi-monthly steamer from New York, an occasional ship from Halifax, and a stray sailing-vessel now and then, puts it quite apart from the thoroughfare of travel. It can never be overrun by a noisy, promiscuous, tumultuous rabble. It must always have the subtile, indefinable charm of remoteness.

The cost of first-cabin passage from New York to Bermuda, including a return ticket good for six months, is $50 in gold. It is a three days' voyage. There being but one line of steamers, there is of course no competition and no choice. On every alternate Thursday during the winter months, the Quebec Steamship Company (A. E. Outerbridge & Co., agents, 51 Broadway) invite you to embark on their staunch little steamer, the Oronoco. You can do so, or you can stay at home. During April, May, and June, when freight is heaviest, the Flamborough runs in connection with the Oronoco, thus making a weekly service and giving the interested tourist a chance to choose between the two. I venture to say that after having made one tour of inspection it will not take him long to decide.

The passage is proverbially disagreeable, but it is not dangerous, and it has the comfort of being short. You may be seasick; indeed, you probably will be. But horribly as you may be rolled about and tossed about in crossing the Gulf Stream, you are in little danger of drowning. The great horror of mid-ocean travel, a collision, is hardly to be thought of, much less dreaded, in the lonely waters through which the gallant little vessels plough their sturdy way; and ere they reach the perilous reefs they are in the hands of trusty pilots, who know the tortuous channels inch by inch.

Connection is made at Bermuda with the Royal Mail steamers for Halifax and Jamaica, which leave monthly.

The expense of living in the islands is of course dependent in a great degree upon individual tastes and habits. In ordinary cases it ranges from $2.00 to $3.50 a day for board and lodging.

The two largest and best hotels in Hamilton are the Hamilton Hotel and the American House; but there are several smaller ones that are said to be comfortable. At St. George's the inns are the Globe and the Bermuda House. Speculators have not yet been induced to build large houses or cottages for the especial use of tourists but in Hamilton, St. George's, Smith's, the Flatts, and Somerset private quarters can be had, and an occasional cottage, furnished or unfurnished. Messrs. Trott & Cox, the Bermuda agents of the Quebec Steamship Company, will furnish all necessary information on these points.

I was told it was possible to obtain fair accommodations in the country for $10 a week, but confess I encountered no one who had made the venture.

The cost of excursions is comparatively trifling. You can get a good horse, carriage, and driver for the trip to St. George's and back — about twenty-four miles in all, and a good day's work — for twelve (English) shillings, or three dollars. Nemo's famous visit to Chubb's Cut, which is farther out than excursionists are apt to go, cost for the whole party of three the enormous sum of eighteen shillings. You can hire a whale-boat and three oarsmen for the day for one pound. You cross the ferry for a penny ha'penny. You pay a shilling or two for a trip on the Moondyne. And you can peep into all the caves you want to for a shilling apiece.

There are no Stewarts or Hoveys in Bermuda, yet by hook or by crook you can get hold of whatever is really necessary in the way of replenishing a dilapidated wardrobe, or supplying yourself with little comforts and conveniences for the person or toilet. American goods, duty included, cost very little more than with us.

English goods are, of course, cheaper. Dressmaking, I was told, was well done, and at fabulously low prices.

My story of Bermudian days is ended. It was our last evening. Trunks were packed, and on the morrow we would be off.

"There is just time for one more row," said Nemo, looking at his watch, and then glancing at the dismantled room. "Put on your bonnet, Lady Mither, and let us go down to the dock and see if we can find Williams."

We found him; and as we glided over the beautiful bay for the last time to the soft dip of plashing oars, our hearts, if not our lips, sang this farewell song to Bermuda and her

WHITE LADY OF THE PROW.

The salt tides ebb, the salt tides flow,
From the near isles the soft airs blow;
From leagues remote, with roar and din,
Over the reefs the waves rush in;
The wild white breakers foam and fret,
Day follows day, stars rise and set;

Yet, grandly poised, as calm and fair
As some proud spirit of the air,
Unmoved she lifts her radiant brow, —
She, the White Lady of the Prow!

The winds blow east, the winds blow west,
From woodlands low to the eagle's nest;
The winds blow north, the winds blow south,
To steal the sweets from the lily's mouth!
We come and go; we spread our sails
Like sea-gulls to the favoring gales,
Or, soft and slow, our oars we dip
Under the lee of the stranded ship.
Yet little recks she when or how,
The grand White Lady of the Prow.

We laugh, we love, we smile, we sigh,
But never she heeds as we glide by, —
Never she cares for our idle ways,
Nor turns from the brink of the world her gaze!
What does she see when her steadfast eyes
Peer into the sunset mysteries,
And all the secrets of time and space
Seem unfolded before her face?
What does she hear when, pale and calm,
She lists for the great sea's evening psalm?

Speak, lady, speak! Thy sealèd lip,
Thou fair white spirit of the ship,
Could tell such tales of high emprise,
Of valorous deeds and counsels wise!
What prince shall rouse thee from thy trance,
And meet thy first revealing glance,
Or what Pygmalion from her sleep
Bid Galatea wake and weep?

The wave's wild passion stirs thee not, —
Oh, is thy life's long love forgot?

How canst thou bear this trancèd calm
By sunlit isles of bloom and balm, —
Thou who hast sailed the utmost seas,
Empress alike of wave and breeze;
Thou who hast swept from pole to pole
Where the great surges swell and roll,
Breasted the billows white with wrath,
Rode in the tempest's fiery path,
And proudly borne to waiting hands
The glorious spoil of farthest lands?

How canst thou bear this silence, deep
And tranquil as an infant's sleep, —
Thou who hast heard above thy head
The white sails sing with wings outspread;
Thou whose strong soul has thrilled to feel
The swift rush of the ploughing keel,
The dash of waves, and the wild uproar
Of ocean lashed from shore to shore?
How canst thou bear this changeless rest,
Thou who hast made the world thy quest?

O Lady of the stranded ship,
Once more our lingering oars we dip
In the clear blue that round thee lies,
Fanned by the airs of Paradise!
Farewell! farewell! But oft when day
On our far hill-tops dies away,
And night's cool winds the pine-trees bow,
Our eyes will see thee, even as now,
Waiting — a spirit pale and calm —
To hear the great sea's evening psalm!

www.ingramcontent.com/pod-product-compliance
Lightning Source LLC
Chambersburg PA
CBHW022127160426
43197CB00009B/1178